Level 2 Diploma for IT Users
for City & Guilds

Spreadsheets

for Office XP

Level
2

Susan Ward

Endorsed by
City&
Guilds

www.heinemann.co.uk
✓ Free online support
✓ Useful weblinks
✓ 24 hour online ordering

01865 888058

Heinemann
Inspiring generations

Heinemann Educational Publishers
Halley Court, Jordan Hill, Oxford OX2 8EJ
Part of Harcourt Education

Heinemann is the registered trademark of
Harcourt Education Limited

First published 2004

07 06 05 04
10 9 8 7 6 5 4 3 2 1

British Library Cataloguing in Publication Data is available
from the British Library on request.

ISBN 0 435 46255 5

Publisher's note

The materials in this Work have been developed by Harcourt Education and the
content and the accuracy are the sole responsibility of Harcourt Education. The City
and Guilds of London Institute accepts no liability whatsoever in respect of any
breach of the intellectual property rights of any third party howsoever occasioned or
damage to the third party's property or person as a result of the use of this Work.

The City & Guilds name and logo are the registered trade marks of The City and
Guilds of London Institute and are used under licence.

Typeset by Tech-Set Ltd, Gateshead, Tyne and Wear
Printed in the UK by Thomson Litho Ltd.

Acknowledgements

The publishers wish to acknowledge that the screenshots in this book have been
reprinted with kind permission from Microsoft Corporation.

Tel: 01865 888058 www.heinemann.co.uk

Contents

Introduction iv

1 Spreadsheet basics 1

2 Spreadsheet layout and formatting 6

3 Editing, copying and further display methods 23

4 Formulas and functions 39

5 Charts and graphs 62

6 Using copy and link to import and extract data 82

7 Printing options 100

8 Spreadsheet design and testing 111

9 Getting help 118

10 Using Excel with other MS Office applications 124

Practice assignments 134

Solutions 141

Outcomes matching guide 149

Quick reference guide 153

Introduction

City & Guilds e-Quals is an exciting new range of IT qualifications developed with leading industry experts. These comprehensive, progressive awards cover everything from getting to grips with basic IT to gaining the latest professional skills.

The range consists of both User and Practitioner qualifications. User qualifications (Levels 1–3) are ideal for those who use IT as part of their job or in life generally, while Practitioner qualifications (Levels 2–3) have been developed for those who need to boost their professional skills in, for example, networking or software development.

e-Quals boasts online testing and a dedicated website with news and support materials and web-based training. The qualifications reflect industry standards and meet the requirements of the National Qualifications Framework.

With e-Quals you will not only develop your expertise, you will gain a qualification that is recognised by employers all over the world.

This spreadsheet unit is organised into five outcomes. You will learn to:
- Design a spreadsheet to meet a given specification
- Create and test a simple spreadsheet
- Link, import and extract data
- Produce graphs and charts
- Export and print spreadsheets

The outcomes matching guide, near the end of the book, gives the outcomes in full and relates each learning point to the section of the book where it is covered. Your tutor will give you a copy of the outcomes, so that you can sign and date each learning point as you master the skills and knowledge.

Before starting work on Spreadsheets Level 2, you should have completed Spreadsheets Level 1, or have equivalent experience of using the Microsoft Excel spreadsheet application.

This book starts with a section that lets you practise the main Level 1 topics to refresh your memory. It then has sections on the Level 2 topics. Each section contains information and practical tasks. There is a detailed method to guide you when you first learn to carry out each task. At the end of a section you will have a chance to practise your skills, check your knowledge, or both. Consolidation exercises provide further practice. Finally you will be able to complete practice assignments, which cover a range of skills and are designed to be similar in style to the City & Guilds assignments for the unit.

There are some solutions to the skills practice and check your knowledge questions at the end of the book. There is also a quick reference section giving methods of carrying out common tasks.

You will need to start at the beginning of the book and work through the sections in order, because some of the tasks in later sections use spreadsheets that are created in earlier sections.

In order to give detailed methods for each task it is necessary to refer to a specific spreadsheet application and operating system, though the City & Guilds unit is not specific and can be completed using any spreadsheet application and operating system. This book refers to Microsoft Excel 2002, which is the spreadsheet application in the Microsoft Office XP suite, and to Microsoft Windows XP.

Section 1 | Spreadsheet basics

You will learn to

- Create a new spreadsheet
- Save a spreadsheet
- Enter text and numbers into spreadsheet cells
- Enter simple formulas and use the SUM function
- Replicate (copy) formulas
- Select cells and alter their formatting
- Modify cell widths
- Print a spreadsheet showing results and showing formulas
- Open a previously prepared spreadsheet
- Edit and delete cell contents
- Save a version of a spreadsheet with a different name

You should already have some experience of using spreadsheets before starting work on Spreadsheets Level 2. You may have completed Level 1, or you may have other equivalent experience.

This section gives you a short revision of the main topics covered at Level 1. The topics should be familiar to you, so this section will have brief reminders rather than full descriptions of the methods.

Pay calculations spreadsheet

You will create a spreadsheet to work out the pay due to hourly paid workers.

Task 1.1	Create and save a spreadsheet and enter data

There are three kinds of entries you can make in spreadsheet cells. These are text (labels), numbers (values) and formulas. This task asks you to enter text and numbers.

Method

1   Start up Excel. A new empty spreadsheet should be created.
2   Save the new spreadsheet with the name **Pay calculations** and Excel will automatically add the extension **.xls** to show that the file contains an Excel spreadsheet.
3   Enter text and number data as shown in Figure 1.1.

4   Enter your name in cell A10.

5   Save the spreadsheet again.

	A	B	C	D	E	F	G	H	I	J
1	**Pay calculations**									
2										
3	**Name**	**Hours**	**Hourly rate**	**Basic pay**	**Bonus**	**Gross pay**	**Nat Ins**	**Tax**	**Deductions**	**Net pay**
4	Avens S	40	£ 6.50					£ 33.68		
5	Bright J	32	£ 7.00					£ 25.76		
6	Chan M	36	£ 6.50					£ 27.96		
7	Fuller L	25	£ 5.50					£ 6.73		
8										
9					**TOTALS**					

Figure 1.1 The Pay calculations spreadsheet

Task 1.2   Enter simple formulas and use the SUM function

You will enter formulas to carry out calculations. The formulas will use the four arithmetic rules – add, subtract, multiply and divide. There is also a formula using the SUM function to add up a column of numbers.

Method

1   In row 4, enter formulas to calculate the basic pay, bonus, gross pay, national insurance, deductions and net pay for S Avens. Calculations are as follows:

Basic pay = Hours * Hourly rate   (**=B4*C4** in cell D4)
Bonus = Basic pay/5   (**=D4/5** in cell E4)
Gross pay = Basic pay + Bonus   (**=D4+E4** in cell F4)
Nat Ins = Gross pay * 10%   (**=F4*10%** in cell G4)
Deductions = Nat Ins + Tax   (**=G4+H4** in cell I4)
Net pay = Gross pay − Deductions   (**=F4−I4** in cell J4)

2   Click in cell D4 to select it. In the bottom right corner of the cell is a black square, the **fill handle**. Point the mouse to the fill handle so that the mouse pointer changes to a black cross. Hold down the left mouse button as you drag the mouse down to cells D5, D6 and D7. The formula from D4 should be copied to D5, D6 and D7.

3   Copy the remaining formulas down to rows 5, 6 and 7 using the fill handle.

4   In cell F9 put in a formula to find the total gross pay for all four employees. Use the SUM function. The formula is: **=SUM(F4:F8)**.

You can use the autosum icon Σ on the toolbar instead of keying in the function.

5   Copy the formula from F9 across to columns G, H, I and J.

6   Save the spreadsheet again.

Remember:

The SUM function is for adding cell contents. Do not try to use it for other kinds of calculation.

Hint:

A **cell reference** identifies a cell by giving its column letter and row number, e.g. **F4**. A **range** of cells is a collection of two or more cells. If the range is a rectangular block of cells, you can refer to it by giving the references of its top left cell and its bottom right cell, separated by a colon, e.g. **F4:F8** or **D6:H9**.

Task 1.3   Select cells and format the contents

Changing the contents of a cell is called editing. Changing the appearance of a cell without changing the contents is called formatting. Suitable formatting can improve the appearance of a spreadsheet and make it easier to use. You will need to use buttons on the Formatting toolbar.

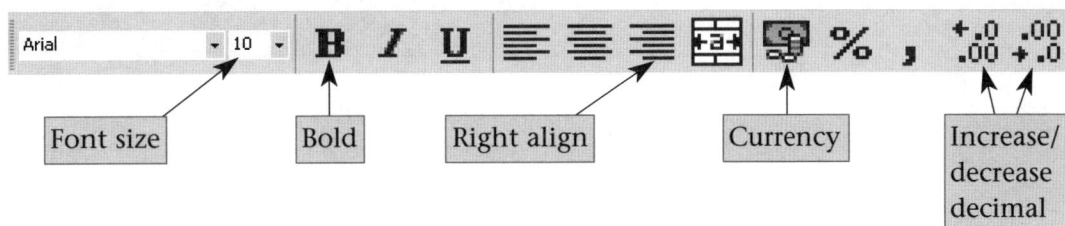

Figure 1.2 Part of the Formatting toolbar

Method

1   Make the text in cell A1 bold and increase the font size to 14.
2   Make the headings in row 3 bold, and right-align the contents except for A3, which should be left aligned.
3   Make cell E9 bold.
4   Cells B4 to B7 should have a number format with no decimal places.
5   Cells C4 to J7 and cells F9 to J9 should have a currency format showing a £ sign and 2 decimal places.
6   Adjust the widths of columns if necessary. Point the mouse to the dividing line between the column letter headings so that the mouse pointer changes to a double arrow. Drag to the right or left.

Task 1.4   Print a spreadsheet showing results and showing formulas

Method

1   Print preview the spreadsheet by using the Print Preview button on the toolbar.
2   You will find that the spreadsheet does not fit on one page. Click the Setup button to show the Page Setup dialogue box. With the Page tab in front, change from portrait to landscape orientation.
3   Print the spreadsheet showing the results.
4   Save the spreadsheet before continuing.
5   Show the formulas on the spreadsheet. You can use the hotkey combination: hold down the Ctrl key and press the ' key. This key is just to the left of the number 1 key on the keyboard. It shows two lines as well as the ' symbol. Alternatively you can use the Tools menu. Select Options, make sure that the View tab is in front, and select the Formulas check box.
6   Print preview and check that all formulas are shown in full.

7 Print the spreadsheet showing the formulas. Let the printout use two sheets of paper if necessary.

8 Close the spreadsheet without saving it again. Close down Excel.

Task 1.5	**Open an existing spreadsheet and edit cell contents**

A major advantage of a computer spreadsheet over calculations on paper is that you can change a value in a cell and the spreadsheet will immediately recalculate its formulas to give the new results.

Method

1 Start up Excel and open your Pay calculations spreadsheet. It should look like Figure 1.3.

	A	B	C	D	E	F	G	H	I	J
1	**Pay calculations**									
2										
3	Name	Hours	Hourly rate	Basic pay	Bonus	Gross pay	Nat Ins	Tax	Deductions	Net pay
4	Avens S	40	£ 6.50	£ 260.00	£ 52.00	£ 312.00	£ 31.20	£ 33.68	£ 64.88	£ 247.12
5	Bright J	32	£ 7.00	£ 224.00	£ 44.80	£ 268.80	£ 26.88	£ 25.76	£ 52.64	£ 216.16
6	Chan M	36	£ 6.50	£ 234.00	£ 46.80	£ 280.80	£ 28.08	£ 27.96	£ 56.04	£ 224.76
7	Fuller L	25	£ 5.50	£ 137.50	£ 27.50	£ 165.00	£ 16.50	£ 6.73	£ 23.23	£ 141.77
8										
9					TOTALS	£ 1,026.60	£ 102.66	£ 94.13	£ 196.79	£ 829.81

Figure 1.3 The Pay calculations spreadsheet with results

2 Save the spreadsheet with the new name of **Pay2.xls.** (File menu, select Save As, key in the new name in the dialogue box.) Continue working with Pay2.xls.

3 M Chan worked for 38 hours, not 36, and the tax figure should be £28.05. Make the corrections. Notice how the results change.

4 Delete your name from cell A10. Key in your name in cell F1 instead.

5 Save the altered spreadsheet.

6 Print the spreadsheet.

7 Save a copy of the spreadsheet on a floppy disk.

8 Close the spreadsheet and close down Excel.

	A	B	C	D	E	F	G	H	I	J
1	**Pay calculations**					S Ward				
2										
3	Name	Hours	Hourly rate	Basic pay	Bonus	Gross pay	Nat Ins	Tax	Deductions	Net pay
4	Avens S	40	£ 6.50	£ 260.00	£ 52.00	£ 312.00	£ 31.20	£ 33.68	£ 64.88	£ 247.12
5	Bright J	32	£ 7.00	£ 224.00	£ 44.80	£ 268.80	£ 26.88	£ 25.76	£ 52.64	£ 216.16
6	Chan M	38	£ 6.50	£ 247.00	£ 49.40	£ 296.40	£ 29.64	£ 28.05	£ 57.69	£ 238.71
7	Fuller L	25	£ 5.50	£ 137.50	£ 27.50	£ 165.00	£ 16.50	£ 6.73	£ 23.23	£ 141.77
8										
9					TOTALS	£ 1,042.20	£ 104.22	£ 94.22	£ 198.44	£ 843.76

Figure 1.4 Altered spreadsheet Pay2.xls

→ Check your knowledge

1 What are the three kinds of entries you can make into a spreadsheet cell?

2 What is the main advantage of a computerised spreadsheet over using a calculator and writing down the results in a grid on paper?

3 What extension does Excel add when you save a spreadsheet file?

4 Which of the following are accepted as numbers?

    A   12.875   D   97cm

    B   £104.50   E   18%

    C   1024a   F   12/05/02

5 Changing the contents stored in a cell is called ...

6 Changing the appearance of a cell without changing the contents is called ...

7 What is a range of cells?

8 Which cells are included in the range C7:E9?

9 What happens to the width of cells if you view the formulas?

10 In Task 1.4 you were asked to save the spreadsheet before viewing formulas and then not to save the spreadsheet again. Why do you think you were asked not to save after viewing formulas?

Section 2

Spreadsheet layout and formatting

You will learn to

- Identify input data, output data and data processing in spreadsheets
- Describe how the design of the spreadsheet and the accuracy of data input impact on the output data
- Create a data capture form
- Apply text enhancements
- Adjust alignment in a cell
- Apply number formats
- Adjust column width and row height
- Apply borders and backgrounds
- Merge cells and centre text, and wrap text in a cell
- Unlock cells and protect spreadsheets

Information: Input, processing and output

Avondale Computers take some of their orders over the phone. The employees in the orders department want to enter the order details directly into a spreadsheet. This spreadsheet should calculate the total cost of the order so that it can be confirmed to the customer over the phone. The order will then be printed out.

Figure 2.1 shows the first draft of the spreadsheet. It is intended for re-use. Details of one order are shown, but these will be deleted after printing and a new order will be entered. You will be creating this spreadsheet later, when you come to Task 2.1.

	A	B	C	D	E	F
1						
2		Avondale Computers				
3						
4			Customer		Order no	298
5		Name	J K Jarvis			
6		Address	34 Holman Drive		Date	12/09/2002
7			Bristol			
8			BS5 2QB		Time	3:00 PM
9		Phone	0770123456			
10						
11						
12		Code	Item description	Unit price	Number	Cost
13		B124	Lexmark Z43 printer	88.41	1	88.41
14		C25	Colour ink cartridge	25.99	1	25.99
15		C26	Black ink cartridge	15.99	2	31.98
16		C54	Paper pack	10.99	2	21.98
17						
18					Subtotal	168.36
19					Carriage	5.00
20					Total	173.36

Figure 2.1 First draft of Avondale Computers order form

Some cells contain labels or constant data that will not be changed on re-use. These cells are: B2, C4, E4, B5, B6, E6, B12, C12, D12, E12, F12, E18, E19, E20, F19.

Some cells contain input data. The computer user will enter fresh data in these cells every time a new order is created. Input data cells are: C5, C6, C7, C8, C9, F4, F6, F8 and the range B13 to E17.

Some cells are for data processing. They contain formulas that carry out calculations. These cells are: F13 to F17, F18, F20. These cells will not be changed on re-use.

Some cells contain the results that are required from the spreadsheet. These cells may also be used for data processing. The most important result from the order form spreadsheet is the total in cell F20. Results, or output data, are intended for display or printing. In the case of the order form, the whole form will be printed. In other cases, only part of a spreadsheet, maybe a summary of results, will be printed.

You should identify labels, input data, processing and output data when you plan a spreadsheet. It is good practice to arrange the input data in one area if possible, so that the spreadsheet user can find the input cells easily. It is often useful to collect output data in one area too, to make a report that can be printed.

The spreadsheet user will expect accurate output. This means that the input data and the processing must be accurate. The spreadsheet designer should make the design as clear as possible in order to help the user to enter data accurately. The processing will be accurate if all the formulas are right.

| Task 2.1 | Create a data capture form for Avondale Computers |

Method

1. Start Excel and create a new spreadsheet.
2. Enter data into the cells as shown in Figure 2.1. The following cells contain formulas: F13 to F17, F18, F20. Make sure that you key in the formulas and not the numbers that are shown as results.
   F13 = D13*E13
   Copy the formula to cells F14, F15, F16 and F17.
   F18 = SUM(F13:F17)
   F20 = F18+F19
3. Check that the formulas produce the results displayed in Figure 2.1. You may find a 0 displayed in cell F17 and 5 instead of 5.00 in cell F19. Do not worry about this difference in display as long as the values in the cells are correct.
4. Save the spreadsheet as **Avondale.xls**. You should save again frequently as you work.

Hint:

Take care to enter data accurately. To pass a spreadsheet assignment, you need 100% accuracy in entering numbers that will be used in calculations.

Information: Formatting

Formatting can make a great improvement in the appearance of a spreadsheet, making it clearer and easier to use. Formatting can be used to distinguish data input areas from other areas, and to emphasise the main results. Some of the methods will be familiar from Level 1. Some will be new. You will be exploring a wider range of formatting methods at Level 2, and there will be more emphasis on the reasons for using formatting.

Task 2.2 | Adjust column width and row height

- Give column C a width of 22.
- Give columns D, E and F widths of 11.
- Give row 2 a height of 21.

Methods for setting the column width

1 Point the mouse to the line between the column heading letters.
2 Hold down the left mouse button and drag the mouse to the right or left. A yellow label appears showing the width so that you can stop when the column is the right width. The label also shows the width in pixels, but this varies from one screen to another.

Or

1 Select the column or any cell in the column. You can select several columns at the same time.
2 Click on the Format menu and select Column from the drop down list, then select Width from the submenu.
3 Key in the chosen width into the dialogue box. Click OK.

Hint:

Perhaps you are wondering how column widths are measured. Column widths are not measured in millimetres or any other standard units. The units of width are based on the number of characters that can fit in a cell, using a particular font size, and a font that has the characters all the same width. You will be using different fonts and sizes so it is unlikely that a cell of width 10 will hold exactly 10 characters in your spreadsheets.

Methods for letting Excel set the column width

Either

1 Point the mouse to the line between the column heading letters. You can select several columns if you wish, then point the mouse to the line between any of their headings.

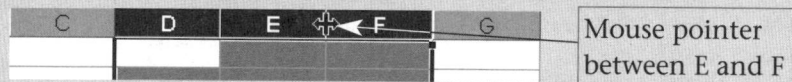

Mouse pointer between E and F

Figure 2.2 Changing the width of several columns

2 Double click on the line. Excel will autofit the column width to display all text in its cells.

Or

1 Select the column or any cell in the column. You can select several columns at the same time.
2 Click on the Format menu, select Column from the drop down list, then select Autofit Selection.

Methods for choosing the row height

Either

1 Point the mouse to the line between the row numbers in the left margin.
2 Hold down the left mouse button and drag the mouse up or down. A yellow label appears showing the height so that you can stop when the row is the right height.

Or

1   Select the row or any cell in the row. You can select several rows at the same time.
2   Click on the Format menu and select Row from the drop down list, then select Height from the submenu.
3   Key in the chosen height into the dialogue box. Click OK.

Task 2.3   Apply text enhancements

Titles and headings are often made bold to emphasise them. Main headings may be enlarged. The font can be changed, but take care to choose fonts that are clear and easy to read.

*   Make the main title of the spreadsheet size 14 bold and dark blue. Change the font from Arial to some other font if you wish.
*   Make the headings in row 12 bold.
*   Make the following cells bold: B5, B6, C4, E4, E6, E18, E19, E20.

Method using toolbar

Font formatting using the toolbar should be familiar from Level 1. You can select cells then use toolbar buttons to change the font and size and to apply bold, italic or underline styles. These toolbar buttons were shown in Figure 1.2 of Section 1 (page 3).

Font colour may be new. Click the arrow beside the font colour button

A ▼ to see a drop down palette of colours. Click on your chosen colour to apply the colour to the font. Clicking on the button itself will apply the most recently used colour.

Method using Format menu

A wider range of options is available from the Format menu.

1   Click on the Format menu to show the drop down list.
2   Select Cells.
3   Click on the Font tab in the Format Cells dialogue box.

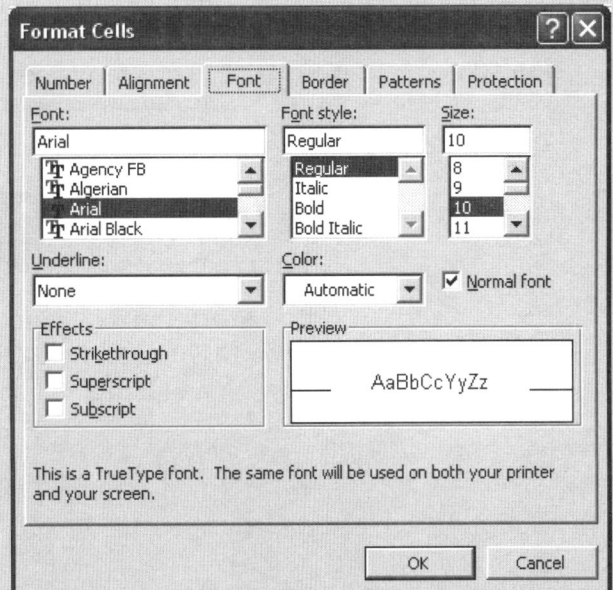

Figure 2.3 Format Cells dialogue box, Font section

In addition to the font, style, size and colour, the dialogue box offers several different kinds of underlining, strikethrough, superscript and subscript. Strikethrough text looks as if it is ~~crossed out~~ . Superscript is small characters above the main text such as the 2 in x^2. Subscript is small characters below the main text, such as the 2 in H_2O.

Information: Number formats

You can format a number in a cell to display as a general number, as a number with a fixed number of decimal places, as currency, as a percentage, as a date or time, and in other ways. Some of these formats should be familiar from Level 1.

The default number format is general number. Numbers are displayed without leading or trailing zeros that do not affect the value of the number. If you key in 012.50 it will be displayed as 12.5.

Some formatting will be applied as you type. For example, you keyed in 12/09/02 into cell F6 of the Avondale spreadsheet. Excel recognises this entry as a date, and formats the cell to display dates. If you key in £30.75 into a cell, the currency format will be applied. If you key in 25%, the percent format will be applied.

The format is for display purposes. The content of the cell, the underlying number that is stored, may not be the same as the display. A date is stored as the number of days since 01/01/1900. In the case of 12/09/02, the number of days is 37511. This stored number can be seen in the cell if you format to general number, or if you switch to formula view. Times are stored as fractions of a day, so that 0.0 is midnight, 0.25 is 6:00 a.m., 0.5 is midday, 0.75 is 6:00 p.m. and so on. A cell displaying 25% is storing the number 0.25. A cell that is formatted to show 2 decimal places will display 5.86 if its stored number is 5.8579. The stored number is used in calculations, not the number shown in the formatted display.

A cell can be formatted as text. This is useful if you want to enter a number, such as a phone number, that should be displayed exactly as you key it in. You cannot use a number in calculations if it is in a cell that is formatted as text.

Task 2.4   Apply number formats

- In the Avondale spreadsheet, leave cells E13 to E16 as general number.
- Format cells D13 to D16 and F13 to F20 to show currency with the £ sign and 2 decimal places.

Method for currency using the toolbar

The quickest method for currency is to use the Formatting toolbar. Select the cells that are to display as currency. Click the Currency button on the toolbar. Adjust the number of decimal places as needed by using the Increase and Decrease decimal buttons.

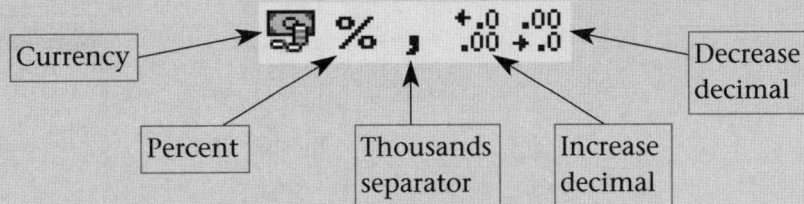

Figure 2.4 Number formats on the Formatting toolbar

Method for currency using the Format menu

The full range of number formats is available from the Format menu.

1   Click the Format menu to show the drop down list.
2   Select Cells.
3   Click on the Number tab in the Format Cells dialogue box if it is not already in front.
4   Select Currency or Accounting from the category list and choose the number of decimal places.

Method for date and time

You will explore the underlying numbers used to display date and time information. You will also try out different date and time formats.

1   Go to cell F6, which displays the date.
2   Click the Format menu and select Cells from the drop down list. The Number tab should be in front.
3   Select General from the category list. Click OK.
4   The number 37511 should be displayed in the cell. Excel starts counting with 1 January 1900 as day 1. 12 September 2002 is day 37511, and 37511 is the number stored in the cell.
5   Click the Format menu and select Cells from the drop down list. The Number tab should be in front.
6   Select Date from the category list.
7   Look at the list of Types to see what date formats are available. As you click on a format, the Sample area shows what would display in the cell. Check that the Locate box is showing English (United Kingdom) because Americans write dates differently. You can show the month as a word, e.g. 14 March 2001, or as a number, e.g. 14/03/2001.
8   You can choose your own format for displaying a date. Select Custom from the category list. See Figure 2.5.

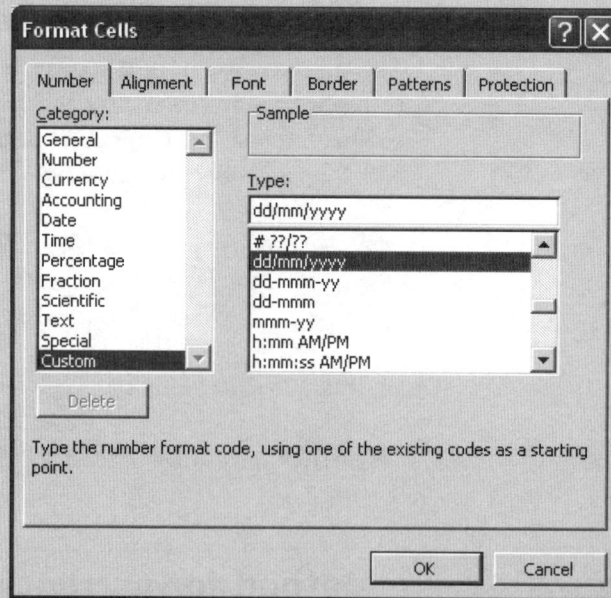

Figure 2.5 Format Cells dialogue box, Number tab in front

9   Scroll down and select dd-mmm-yy from the Type list. This will produce a date with the month shown in a short form, e.g. 14-Mar-02. Click OK.
10   Go to cell E8 and key in **Time**.
11   Go to cell F8 and key in **15:00**. Make sure that you have a colon (:) after the 15. Excel recognises this entry as a time of day.
12   Click the Format menu and select Cells from the drop down list. The Number tab should be in front.
13   Click on the General category and look at the Sample area of the dialogue box. You should see 0.625. Excel saves times as fractions of a day.
14   Click on the Time category and explore the time formats. As you click on a format, the Sample area will show what would appear in the cell.
15   Select the format that will show the time as 3:00 PM. Click OK.

Method for text

1   Go to cell B9 and key in **Phone**.
2   Go to cell C9 and key in **0770123456**.
3   The number should appear with the leading 0 missing, and right aligned in the cell. This is not what you want for a phone number. The leading 0 has to be included. Delete the entry in cell C9.
4   With cell C9 selected, click the Format menu and select Cells from the drop down list. The Number tab should be in front.
5   Select Text from the category list and click OK.
6   In cell C9, key in **0770123456**.
7   This time the leading 0 should be shown, and the entry should be left aligned. Excel has treated the entry as text and displayed it exactly as you keyed it in.
8   Save the spreadsheet.

Hint:

Instead of formatting cell C9 to text, you could key in '**0770123456** starting with a single quote. The single quote makes Excel treat the entry as text. The quote is not displayed.

Information: More number formats

Excel provides some additional number formats that are not required by the City & Guilds outcomes for Spreadsheets Level 2. You might like to explore them if you have time, but you will not be expected to use them at Level 2. You might like to open a new spreadsheet for your experiments rather than using your Avondale spreadsheet. There is no need to save this new spreadsheet.

Fractions

This format shows numbers as fractions in the form $\frac{1}{2}$, $\frac{3}{4}$, $1\frac{1}{4}$, etc. To try it out:

- Key in 0.5 in a spare spreadsheet cell. Select this cell.
- Click on the Format menu and select Cells. With the Number tab in front, select 'Fraction' from the Category list. Keep the default type 'Up to one digit'. Click OK.

Try keying in other decimal numbers such as 0.75, 1.25, etc. and formatting them to fraction. You could try a few calculations using fractions. When you have finished, clear the cells and format them back to general number.

Scientific

Scientists and engineers often use very large or very small numbers. It is not convenient to write out these numbers in the normal way, so there is a special way of writing them called scientific or exponential notation. A full explanation is outside the scope of this book, but here is a taster.

- Key in 25000000 in a spare spreadsheet cell. Select this cell.
- Click on the Format menu and select Cells. With the Number tab in front, select 'Scientific' from the Category list. Keep the default type. Click OK.

The display shows as 2.50E+07. The 2.50 comes from the original number, but has a decimal point after the first digit. E stands for exponential. +07 means that you would multiply by 10000000 (1 followed by 7 zeros) to get back to the original number. You could try keying in other very large numbers and converting them to scientific format. When you have finished, clear the cells you have used and format them back to general number.

Special

There are no special formats for the UK. Special formats for the US include US zip codes, phone numbers and social security numbers.

Custom

This category lets you create your own formats for special purposes by using codes to control the display of numbers. You have already seen that the code dd/mmm/yy produces a date in the form 14-Mar-02. You might like to try putting a date in a cell and formatting it with a custom format of dd-mm-yyyy. Then try dd mmmm yy to show the month in full. Then try dd mmmm yyyy to show the year in full as well. These last two options are not on the list, but you can key them in yourself. If you have been using a new spreadsheet for your experiments, you can now close it. There is no need to save it.

Task 2.5 | Adjust alignment in a cell

In the Avondale Computer Supplies spreadsheet, right align the labels in cells D12, E12, F12.

Method

I Select the cells and click the Right Align button on the Formatting toolbar. This should be familiar from Level I.

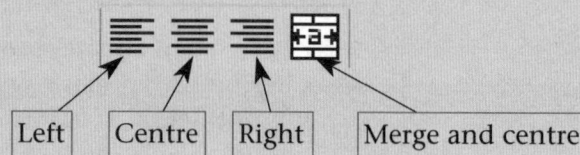

Figure 2.6 Alignment buttons on the Formatting toolbar

Task 2.6 | Merge cells and centre text

Centre the title Avondale Computers across the top of the invoice form.

Method

1 Select cells B2 to F2.
2 Click the Merge and Centre button on the Formatting toolbar.

This merges the five selected cells so that they behave as one cell. The title is centred across all five merged cells.

Information: More alignment options

More alignment options are available from the Format Cells dialogue box. To see these, select Cells from the Format menu as usual. Click on the Alignment tab in the Format Cells dialogue box.
The Alignment section offers:

- Horizontal alignment in a cell, including the usual left, centre and right.
- Indent within a cell. If you want a space at the left of the cell before the text starts, use this indent rather than using the space bar.
- Vertical alignment, bottom, centre or top of a tall cell.
- Orientation. You can have text displayed vertically in a cell, or at an angle. Key in the number of degrees for the angle, or drag the marker round the scale.
- Wrap text where it is too long to fit into a cell.
- Shrink text to fit into a cell.
- Merge selected cells so that they behave as one cell. →

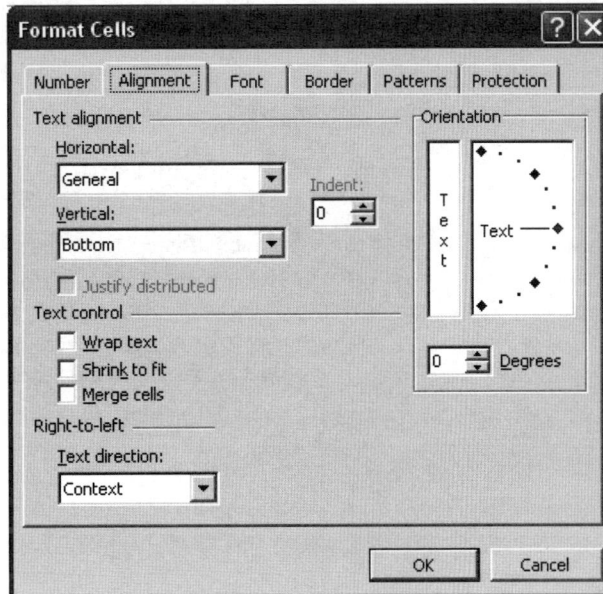

Figure 2.7 Format Cells dialogue box, Alignment section

You will wrap text in the next task. Meanwhile you might like to try out some of the other alignment options using a new spreadsheet. Orientation is fun to try, and is useful if you need headings for narrow columns. Return to your Avondale Computer spreadsheet when you have finished experimenting.

Task 2.7 — Wrap text in a cell

Method

1. Select cell C16.
2. Replace the text 'Paper pack' with 'Pack of 100 sheets A4 paper 80g weight'. The text should be too long to display fully in the cell.
3. With cell C16 selected, click on the Format menu to show the drop down list.
4. Select Cells so that the Format Cells dialogue box shows.
5. Click on the Alignment tab if it is not already in front.
6. Click on the check box labelled 'Wrap text' to place a tick.
7. Click OK.

Hint:

You can start a new line when you are entering text into a cell with wrapped text. Hold down the Alt key as you press the Enter key to start the new line.

The text should wrap in the cell so that it is all displayed. Row 16 should become taller to allow this.

Method

1 Select cells B1 to F21.
2 Click on the Format menu to show the drop down list.
3 Select Cells so that the Format Cells dialogue box is displayed.
4 Click on the Border tab to bring it to the front. See Figure 2.8.

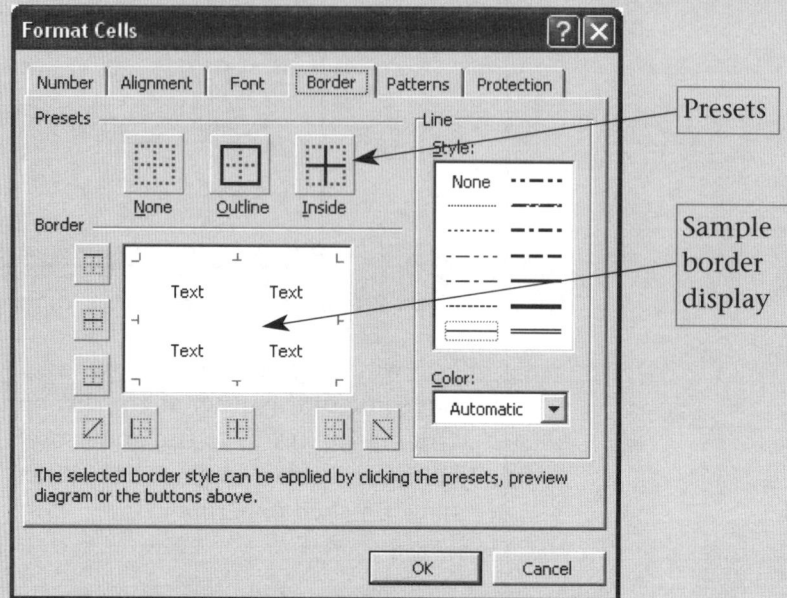

Figure 2.8 Format Cells dialogue box, Border section

5 In the Presets section at the top, click Outline.
6 An outline border appears in the sample border display in the Border area of the dialogue box.
7 Click OK.
8 Deselect the cells so that you can see the effect of the border. It does not show up well at present because of the gridlines.
9 Select cells B12 to F16.
10 Display the Format Cells dialogue box again.
11 In the Presets section, click Outline then click Inside.
12 Outline and inner borders appear in the sample border display in the Border area of the dialogue box.
13 Click OK.
14 Deselect the cells to see the borders.
15 Select cells E18 to F20.
16 Apply outline and inside borders to these cells.

Information: Borders

There are more options in the Border section of the Format Cells dialogue box.

To remove borders you can click the None preset.   →

You can put in lines one at a time by clicking the Border buttons or by clicking directly into the sample border display.

You can choose thicker or thinner lines or dashed lines from the Style area before you apply borders. You can also choose a colour for the lines.

You have plenty of choice in applying borders, but it is usually best to keep your design simple.

Some of the more common border options are available from the Formatting toolbar. Click the arrow next to the Borders button to see the options, then click on your chosen option. The most recently used option is displayed as the Borders button. To apply this option you can just click the button.

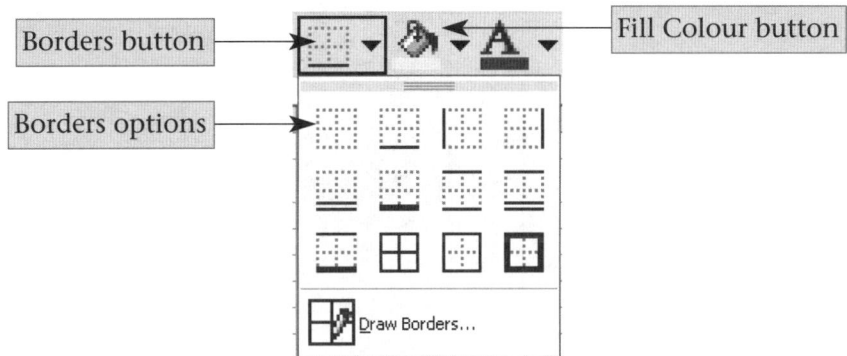

Figure 2.9 Borders button with options

Task 2.9   Apply backgrounds and patterns

You can apply a coloured background to cells. This is not just for decoration. It can be useful in showing which cells are intended for data entry and which are not.

Method

I	Select cells AI to G23.
2	Click the arrow beside the Fill Colour button on the Formatting toolbar.
3	Select a light blue from the colour palette.
4	Select cells C5 to C9. These are the data input cells for the customer name and address.
5	Click the arrow beside the Fill Colour button on the Formatting toolbar.
6	Click No Fill so that the background colour disappears from the cells.
7	Select cells F4, F6, F8 and B13 to E16. Hold down the Ctrl key as you select cells that are not adjacent.
8	The Fill Colour button should be displaying the No Fill option that you used last time. Click on the button to remove the background colour from the selected cells.

Information: Fills and patterns

Background fill colours are available from the Patterns section of the Format Cells dialogue box. There is also a drop down list labelled Pattern. You can choose a pattern of stripes or dots using two colours. Be very sparing in your use of this option. Avoid using it in cells that contain data because the data will be difficult to read.

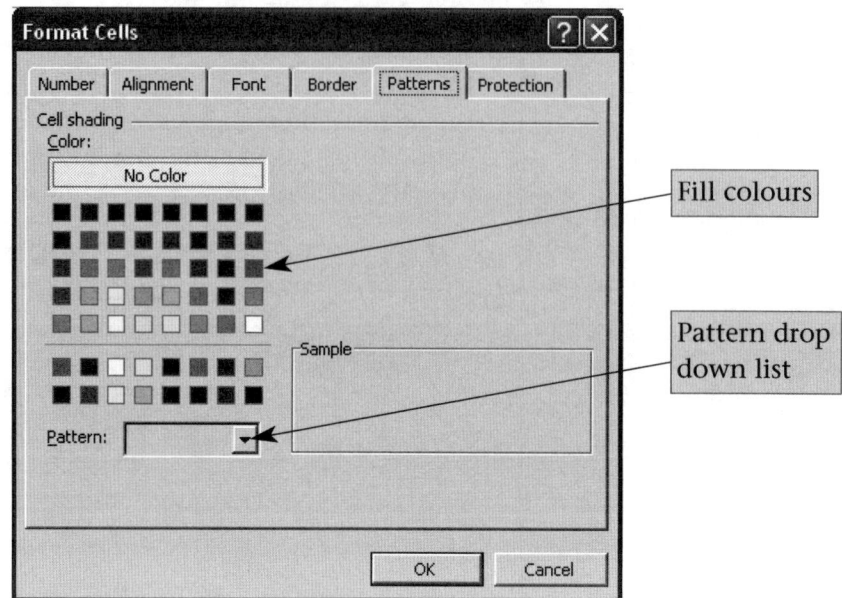

Figure 2.10 Format Cells dialogue box, Patterns section

Remember:

Are you saving your work after each successful change?

Information: Protecting spreadsheets and unlocking cells

Spreadsheets may be used and reused many times. A spreadsheet may be used not by the person who created the spreadsheet, but by inexperienced people who do not understand how to set up formulas. It is important that the spreadsheet users enter their input data in the right cells and do not key in anything in cells that are not supposed to be changed. In particular, they must not key in anything in cells that contain formulas.

Excel has a protection feature to stop users from accidentally ruining a spreadsheet by entering data in the wrong places. By default the protection is off so that you can enter data in any cell. Before switching the protection on, you must decide which cells may be changed and which cells must not be changed. The data input cells need to be unlocked and all the other cells should be locked. When protection is on, unlocked cells can be changed but locked cells cannot. By default, all cells are formatted as locked.

You set up your spreadsheet and complete all the formatting. You unlock the input cells and leave the others locked. Finally, you switch on the protection so that the locking of cells takes effect. →

You can put a password on the protection of a spreadsheet. Nobody can take the protection off unless they know the password. If you forget the password then there is no way that you can change the design of the spreadsheet again. A password can be useful if you are setting up a spreadsheet for other people and you do not want them to meddle with the design. Otherwise it is safer not to use a password in case you forget it.

Task 2.10   Unlock data input cells and protect a spreadsheet

Method

1   Select cells C5 to C9.
2   Click the Format menu to show the drop down list.
3   Select Cells to show the Format Cells dialogue box.
4   Click on the Protection tab. See Figure 2.11.
5   Click in the check box labelled Locked to remove the tick.
6   Click OK.

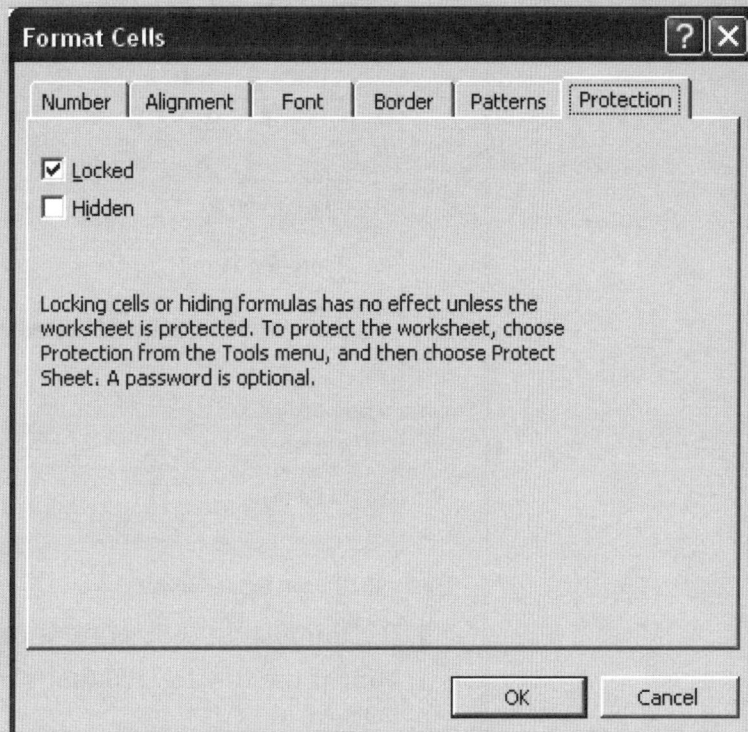

Format Cells   [?][X]

| Number | Alignment | Font | Border | Patterns | Protection |

☑ Locked
☐ Hidden

Locking cells or hiding formulas has no effect unless the worksheet is protected. To protect the worksheet, choose Protection from the Tools menu, and then choose Protect Sheet. A password is optional.

OK   Cancel

Figure 2.11 Format Cells dialogue box, Protection section

7   Select cells F4, F6, F8 and cells B13 to E16.
8   Unlock these cells in the same way.
9   Click the Tools menu to show the drop down list.
10   Select Protection then select Protect Sheet from the submenu.
11   The Protect Sheet dialogue box appears. It invites you to enter a password. Do not enter anything. Just click OK.

The Protection section of the Format Cells dialogue box has a Hidden option as well as a Locked option. Selecting Hidden does not hide cell contents as the name might suggest. If the sheet is protected, hidden cells will display their results as normal, but formulas will not be shown in formula view. It is the formulas that are hidden, not the results. To hide results, you need to hide a whole row or column. This will come in the next section.

Remember:

Take regular breaks. This could be a good time to take a break.

12   Try to enter 3 in cell E14. This should be successful because the cell is unlocked.

13   Try to enter data in any of the locked cells. There should be an error message.

14   Look at the Formatting toolbar. Most of the buttons should be greyed out. Try out any of the buttons. You should find that they do not work. You cannot format a protected worksheet.

15   Save your spreadsheet.

16   Preview and print your spreadsheet.

→ **Practise your skills 2.1:** Food survey spreadsheet

For this you will set up a spreadsheet that will be used by an interviewer in a survey about food. The interviewer will ask how many portions of fruit and vegetables a person eats in a week.

If you cannot remember the methods, look back at the tasks earlier in this section.

1   Load Excel if it is not already open.

2   Create a new spreadsheet as shown in Figure 2.12 and call it **Food Survey.xls.**

	A	B	C	D	E
1	**Food Survey**				
2					
3	**Interviewer name**	Your name			
4	**Interviewer ID**	FS103			
5					
6	**Name (optional)**	G Bailey			
7					
8	**On average, how many times a week do you eat:**				
9	Apples	3		Potatoes	4
10	Oranges	1		Carrots	2
11	Bananas	2		Cabbage	0
12	Grapes	0		Peas	3
13	Other fruit	2		Beans	1
14	**Total fruit**			Other vegetables	5
15				**Total vegetables**	

Figure 2.12 Food Survey spreadsheet

3   Put formulas in cells B14 and E15 to work out the totals.

4   Format the title to Arial font size 16 bold. Centre the title across cells A1 to E1.

5   Make the following cells bold: A3, A4, A6, A8, A14, B14, D15, E15.

6   Put an outline border round cells A1 to E16.

7   Put an outline and inner borders round cells A9 to B14 and D9 to E15.

8   Put a shaded background in cells A1 to E16 except for the data input cells, which should be left with a clear background.

9   Unlock the data input cells and protect the spreadsheet.   →

10 Clear the input data and enter a new set of data. P Latimer eats 5 apples and 1 orange a week, and eats potatoes 6 times, carrots 4 times and peas 5 times.

11 Check that you cannot enter data into the locked cells.

12 Save the spreadsheet and print a copy.

→ **Practise your skills 2.2:** Clinic appointments spreadsheet

You will set up a spreadsheet to record appointments at a hospital clinic.

1 Load Excel if it is not already open.

2 Create a new spreadsheet as shown in Figure 2.13 and call it **Clinic.xls.**

	A	B	C
1		Avondale Hospital	
2			
3		Clinic Appointment	
4			
5		Patient name	Mrs J Welland
6		Patient address	3 Greenlea Close
7			Avondale
8			Avon
9			BS23 4HD
10			
11		Patient phone	01122 654321
12			
13		Name of clinic	Fractures
14		Consultant	Dr Varju
15		Appointment date	25/10/2002
16		Appointment time	11:00
17		Reference no.	12874
18			
19			
20		If you are unable to keep this appointment	
21		please phone 01122 123456	

Figure 2.13 Clinic spreadsheet

3 Format the title to Arial font size 14 bold. Centre the title across cells B1 to D1.

4 Make cell B3 bold.

5 Put an outline border round cells B1 to D21.

6 Put an outline and inner borders round cells C5 to C9 and cells C13 to C17.

7 Put an outline border round cell C11.

8 Put a light coloured background in cells B1 to D21 except for the data input cells, which should be left with a clear background. You may need to make text bold if it does not show up well against the coloured background.

9 Unlock the data input cells and protect the spreadsheet. →

10 Clear the input data and enter a new set of data. The appointment is for Mrs H Ormerod of 3 Ranwell Drive, Avondale, Avon, BS23 6GS. Her phone number is 01122 666333. She has an appointment to visit the ante-natal clinic, consultant Mr Williams, on 29/10/02 at 9:30. The reference number is 12913.

11 Check that you cannot enter data into the locked cells.

12 Save the spreadsheet and print a copy.

→ Check your knowledge

To answer questions 1–4, look back at the Pay calculations spreadsheet that you created in Section 1.

1 Which are the data input cells in the Pay calculations spreadsheet?

2 Which cells contain labels that are not changed?

3 Which cells are for calculations?

4 Which cells display results?

5 Can you change the data in a cell if the cell is locked and the worksheet is unprotected?

6 Can you change the data in a cell if the cell is unlocked and the worksheet is unprotected?

7 Can you change the data in a cell if the cell is locked and the worksheet is protected?

8 Can you change the data in a cell if the cell is unlocked and the worksheet is protected?

9 By default, are cells locked or unlocked?

10 By default, are worksheets protected or unprotected?

11 A cell displays the date 13/09/02 (13 September 2002). What is the underlying number stored in the cell? **Hint:** Look at the methods for date and time in Task 2.4 (pages 11–12).

12 A cell contains the number 0.75. The cell is then formatted to display time. What time will it show?

Section 3

Editing, copying and further display methods

You will learn to

- Use the fill handle to copy and to increment
- Copy cell contents
- Move cell contents
- Copy cell formatting
- Delete cell contents and clear formatting
- Insert and delete rows and columns and insert copied cells
- Use search and replace to edit cells
- Hide cells
- Freeze windows and split windows
- Use headers and footers
- Print with/without repeated table headings
- Print gridlines, column letters and row numbers

Task 3.1 — Start creating the Computer Supplies spreadsheet

You will create a spreadsheet to show a list of customers of a computer supplies company, and the items that the customers have bought.

Method

1. Create a new spreadsheet as shown in Figure 3.1. Cell G4 should contain the formula =E4*F4.
2. Format cell A1 to bold, font size 16.
3. Make the headings in row 3 bold.
4. Save the spreadsheet with the name **Computer Supplies.xls**.

	A	B	C	D	E	F	G
1	**Computer Supplies**						
2							
3	Order date	Customer ID	Customer Name	Item description	Unit price	Number ordered	Value of order
4	24/06/2002	2001	Mr K Smithers	Monitor SDM M51	492.33	1	492.33
5							
6							
7							
8							
9							
10							
11							

Figure 3.1 Starting the Computer Supplies spreadsheet

Task 3.2 — Use the fill handle to copy and to increment

You have used the fill handle before, but now you will explore it in more detail.

Method

1 Select cell A4 so that the fill handle appears in the bottom right corner of the cell.
2 Drag the fill handle down to cell A10.
3 You should find that the date is not copied exactly, but is **incremented**. One extra day is added each time the cell is copied. This is shown in Figure 3.2. Excel is normally set up to increment dates when they are copied in this way.

3	Order date	Cus
4	24/06/2002	
5	25/06/2002	
6	26/06/2002	
7	27/06/2002	
8	28/06/2002	
9	29/06/2002	
10	30/06/2002	
11		

Figure 3.2 Using the fill handle with dates

4 Delete the contents of cells A5 to A10. In this spreadsheet we want the date copied exactly and not incremented.
5 Select cell A4, which should still contain the date 24/06/02.
6 Hold down the Ctrl key on the keyboard as you use the mouse to drag the fill handle down to cell A10. Let go of the mouse button before you let go of the Ctrl key. You should see a little + sign beside the mouse pointer as you drag.
7 Check that this time the date 24/06/02 is in each cell.
8 Select cell B4. It should contain the number 2001.
9 Use the fill handle to drag down to cell B10.
10 You should find that all the cells contain the number 2001. Excel normally copies ordinary numbers and does not increment them.
11 Delete the contents of cells B5 to B10.
12 Select cell B4 again.
13 Hold down the Ctrl key on the keyboard as you drag the fill handle down to cell B10.
14 This time the number should be incremented as it is copied. Your spreadsheet should now look like Figure 3.3.

Hint:

A little icon appears at the bottom right of the range of cells you have filled. Point the mouse to this icon to see an arrow. Click the arrow to see a drop down list. You can choose a normal copy or a 'fill series' copy that increments the values.

3	Order date	Customer ID	Cus
4	24/06/2002	2001	Mr
5	24/06/2002	2002	
6	24/06/2002	2003	
7	24/06/2002	2004	
8	24/06/2002	2005	
9	24/06/2002	2006	
10	24/06/2002	2007	
11			

Figure 3.3 The copied order dates and customer IDs

15 Save the spreadsheet.

16 Before continuing with the spreadsheet, explore the fill handle further. Go to cell C16 and key in **Monday**. Drag the fill handle down to cell C22. You should see all the days of the week. Try dragging the fill handle to the right. Try dragging to the left. Try dragging up. Delete all the days of the week so that the spreadsheet is back in the state it was when you saved it.

Task 3.3 — Copy cell contents and continue entering data

Three other customers have bought the same monitor as Mr Smithers. To save keying in, you can copy the details of the monitor from row 4 to other rows.

Method

1 Enter the remaining customer names as shown in column C of Figure 3.4. Do not key in any other data at this stage.

	A	B	C	D	E	F	G
1	**Computer Supplies**						
2							
3	Order date	Customer ID	Customer Name	Item description	Unit price	Number ordered	Value of order
4	24/06/2002	2001	Mr K Smithers	Monitor SDM M51	492.33	1	492.33
5	24/06/2002	2002	Ms B Coates	Monitor Relisys	128.08	1	128.08
6	24/06/2002	2003	Mr F Hussein	Monitor 520F	374.83	1	374.83
7	24/06/2002	2004	Mr P Ibrahim	Monitor SDM M51	492.33	1	492.33
8	24/06/2002	2005	Ms D Jameson	Monitor SDM M51	492.33	1	492.33
9	24/06/2002	2006	Mr V Webb	Monitor 705D	158.93	2	317.86
10	24/06/2002	2007	Mr L Wilson	Monitor SDM-M51	492.33	1	492.33

Figure 3.4 More data for the Computer Supplies spreadsheet

2 Select cells D4 to G4.

3 Give the copy command by clicking the Copy button on the toolbar 📋. A flashing dotted line, the **marquee**, appears round the cells you have chosen to copy. The contents of the cells are copied to a special temporary storage area called the clipboard.

4 Select cell D7.

5 Give the paste command by clicking the Paste button on the toolbar 📋 ▾. The contents of the copied cells appear in cells D7 to G7. You could have selected cells D7 to G7 before pasting, but it is not necessary. It is simpler just to select the first cell in the range of cells where you want to paste.

6 Select cell D8.

7 Give the paste command again.

8 Select cell D10.

9 Give the paste command again. Once you have an item copied to the clipboard, you can paste it as many times as you like. A little Paste icon appears after pasting and gives you a choice of Paste options. Ignore it for now.

10 Enter the remaining data in columns D, E and F as shown in Figure 3.4.

11 Use the fill handle to copy the formula from cell G4 down the column to cell G10.

12 Save the spreadsheet.

Information: Copy, paste, cut and the clipboard

The copy command takes a copy of the contents of the selected cells and stores it temporarily on the clipboard. The original cells keep their contents. There are several ways of giving the copy command.

- Use the toolbar Copy button.
- Click on the Edit menu and select Copy from the drop down list.
- Right click on the selected area and select Copy from the pop-up menu.
- Hold down the Ctrl key as you press the c key.

Excel puts a marquee round the copied cells. As long as the marquee is present, the cell contents are available for pasting. If you carry out some other action, such as saving the file or entering data in another cell, the marquee disappears and you can no longer paste the cell contents. This copying behaviour is different from the behaviour you may have met in other applications such as MS Word, where you can still paste after carrying out other actions.

The cut command also puts a copy of the selected cells on the clipboard and puts a marquee round the selected cells. After the selection has been pasted, the contents of the original cells are deleted. Cut and paste is therefore a way of moving cell contents. The cutting behaviour of Excel is also rather different from the behaviour of Word. In Word, text disappears immediately if you cut. In Excel the cell contents stay in place within the marquee until you paste. There are several ways of giving the cut command.

- Use the toolbar Cut button.
- Click on the Edit menu and select Cut from the drop down list.
- Right click on the selected area and select Cut from the pop-up menu.
- Hold down the Ctrl key as you press the x key.

The paste command puts the item from the clipboard into cells on the spreadsheet, starting with the selected cell. You can select a range of cells for pasting, but the selection must have the same number of rows and columns as the range that was copied or cut. There are several ways of giving the paste command.

- Use the toolbar Paste button.
- Click on the Edit menu and select Paste from the drop down list.
- Right click on the selected area and select Paste from the pop-up menu.
- Hold down the Ctrl key as you press the v key.

Older versions of Excel allowed only one item on the clipboard at a time. Excel 2002 shares a new clipboard with other MS Office applications. You can copy or cut up to 12 items and paste them in any order by selecting them from the clipboard. To show the clipboard, click on the Edit menu and select Office Clipboard. The clipboard appears on the right of the screen and shows the items available for pasting. You click on an item to paste it in.

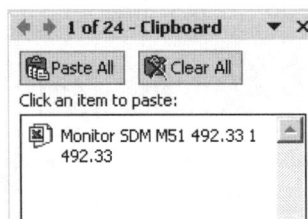

Figure 3.5 The clipboard

Task 3.4   Move cell contents

You have copied text, numbers and formulas from one cell to another, leaving the original cell contents in place. Next you will move the contents from one set of cells to another. You could do this using the cut and paste commands, but instead you will use the drag and drop method.

Method

1	Select cell A4.
2	Point the mouse to the centre of the cell. The pointer looks like a large white cross. Point the mouse at the fill handle. The pointer looks like a small black cross. Point the mouse at the edge of the cell. The pointer looks like a white arrow pointing to crossed arrows.

3	Order date
4	24/06/02
5	24/06/02

Figure 3.6 Arrow pointer ready for drag and drop

3	When the pointer is a white arrow, hold down the left mouse button and drag the mouse to cell A11, then release the button. The contents of cell A4 move to cell A11.
4	Select cells B4 to G4.
5	Point the mouse at the outer edge of the selection so that the mouse pointer looks like a white arrow. Hold down the left mouse button and drag the cell contents down to cells B11 to G11, then drop them by releasing the button.
6	Row 4 should now be empty, and the details of Mr Smithers' purchase are now in row 11.
7	Save the spreadsheet.

Information: Using the drag and drop method to copy

Drag and drop is normally used to move cell contents, leaving the original cells empty. If you hold down the Ctrl key as you drag and drop, you will make a copy of the cell contents. The original cells will be unchanged. Take care to release the mouse button before you release the Ctrl key. A little + sign appears by the mouse pointer as you drag, showing that you are making a copy.

Drag and drop can be quicker than copy and paste, but it needs good mouse control. It is a convenient method if the original cells and the destination cells are visible on the screen at the same time. If you need to scroll to show the destination cells then it may be easier to use copy and paste.

Normally drag and drop has the same effect as cut and paste, while drag and drop with Ctrl has the same effect as copy and paste, but there are some exceptions. When you move cells containing formulas, the cell references may behave differently. After moving cells with formulas, check that the formulas still refer to the right cells.

Task 3.5 — Copy cell formatting

If you have set up a cell with a particular format – font, number, borders, coloured background, etc. – you may want to copy that format to another cell without copying the cell contents. A quick way of copying formats is to use the Format Painter, and that is the method we use here.

Method

1	Go to cell E1 and enter the text **Order List**. The entry should appear in the default format of Arial font size 10.
2	Click on cell A1 to select it. This cell should contain the heading in size 16, bold font.
3	Click the Format Painter button on the main toolbar. This picks up the format from the selected cell A1. Notice that a little brush picture appears beside the mouse pointer and the button looks as if it is pressed in
4	Click on cell E1 to select it. This cell should now have the same format as cell A1. The Format Painter button and the mouse pointer return to normal.

> **Hint:**
>
> If you want to copy a format to several non-adjacent cells, you can double click the Format Painter button. It will remain active and pressed in so that you can apply the format as many times as you like. Click the Format Painter button again to switch it off.

You have applied a format to a single cell, E1. You could apply the format to a range of adjacent cells by selecting them all.

Task 3.6 — Delete cell contents and clear formatting

You already know how to delete the contents of a cell by pressing the Delete key on the keyboard. The Delete key will not remove the formatting of a cell. There are various menu options for clearing contents and formatting from a cell.

Method

1	Select cell E1.
2	Click on the Edit menu and select Clear from the drop down list.
3	You now have four choices from the submenu. These are: All, Formats, Contents and Comments. Select Formats.
4	The format of cell E1 should return to the default of Arial size 10, not bold. The contents of the cell are unchanged.
5	Use the Format Painter button to re-apply the formatting of cell A1 to cell E1.
6	With cell E1 selected, click on the Edit menu and select Clear from the drop down list.
7	Select All from the submenu.
8	The contents and the formatting should both be cleared from cell E1.

Selecting Contents from the submenu would have the same effect as pressing the Delete key on the keyboard. It clears the contents but not the formats.

Task 3.7 — Insert and delete rows and columns

You will insert a new row, move some data to the new row, then delete an empty row. This method can be used for arranging rows in a different order.

Method

1	Select cell A9. (Or any cell in row 9 would do.)
2	Click on the Insert menu and select Rows from the drop down list.
3	A new empty row appears. All the rows below it are moved down and renumbered.
4	Select cells A6 to G6. Move the contents of these cells to the new row 9. (Use cut and paste or drag and drop.) This should leave row 6 empty.
5	Select cell A6. (Or any cell in row 6 would do.)
6	Click on the Edit menu and select Delete from the drop down list.
7	The Delete dialogue box appears. Select the Entire Row option and click OK. The row is deleted. All the lower rows are moved up and renumbered.

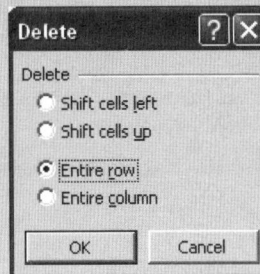

Figure 3.7 Delete dialogue box

8	Select cell D1. (Or any cell in column D would do.)
9	Click on the Insert menu and select Columns.
10	A new column D is inserted and columns are moved to the right and given new letters to leave space for it.
11	Enter data in the new column D as shown in Figure 3.8.

C	D
es	
Customer Name	Credit OK?
Ms B Coates	Yes
Mr P Ibrahim	Yes
Ms D Jameson	Yes
Mr F Hussein	Yes
Mr V Webb	No
Mr L Wilson	Yes
Mr K Smithers	Yes

Figure 3.8 Data for the new column D

12	Save the spreadsheet.

Information: Variations on inserting and deleting

You do not have to delete a complete row at a time. In the Delete dialogue box, you can choose to delete only the selected cell(s) and move other cells to the left or up to fill in the gap.

You can delete the column(s) containing your selected cell(s). Select 'Entire column' in the Delete dialogue box.

You could select an entire row by clicking on its row number. Edit – Delete will then delete the row without showing the Delete dialogue box. If you select an entire column by clicking on its column letter, Edit – Delete will delete the column without showing the dialogue box.

You can select several rows or columns and delete them in one operation. You can also select several rows or columns before you give the command to Insert. If you have selected three rows then three new rows will be inserted, and so on.

Task 3.8   Insert copied cells

If you paste into cells that contain data, then you will lose the existing data. In Task 3.7 you pasted into an empty row so that you did not lose data. An alternative method creates a new row and pastes data into it in one operation.

Method

1   Select cells A7 to H7.
2   Give the copy command by any method of your choice.
3   Select cell A9.
4   Click the Insert menu and select Copied Cells from the drop down list. (Copied Cells is not normally on the list. It appears when there is data on the clipboard and the marquee is still round the copied cells.)
5   The Insert Paste dialogue box appears. Make sure that 'Shift cells down' is selected and click OK.
6   A new row 9 is inserted and your copied cells are pasted in. Check that this has happened correctly.
7   Delete row 9 so that the spreadsheet is returned to its state before Task 3.8.

You will use the search and replace facility to change the information about one of the monitors.

Method

1. Select cell AI. This lets you start the search from the beginning of the spreadsheet.
2. Click on the Edit menu and select Replace. The Replace dialogue box appears.

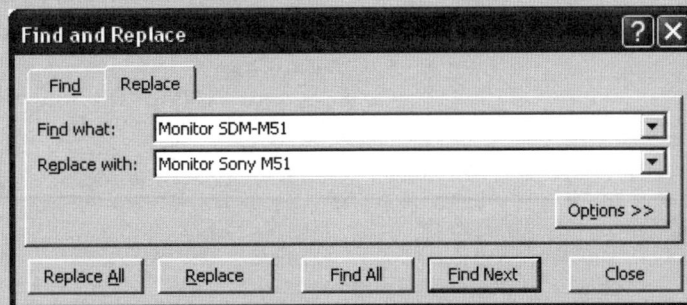

Figure 3.9 Replace dialogue box

3. In the 'Find what' box, key in **Monitor SDM-M51**.
4. In the 'Replace with' box, key in **Monitor Sony M51**.
5. There is no need to change the other options but click the Options button to see what they are. You can find and replace formats as well as data, and can search one sheet or the whole workbook. You can choose to search by rows or by columns. By default capital letters are ignored in the search, but you can choose to match the case of the letters. By default your text will be found if it occurs anywhere in a cell, but you can choose to match it against the contents of entire cells.
6. Click the 'Find next' button. Cell E6 should be selected. Move the Replace dialogue box if it hides cell E6.
7. Click the Replace button.
8. The text in cell E6 should be replaced and cell E7 should be selected.
9. Keep clicking the Replace button until the text has been replaced every time it occurs. When there is no more text to find, you should see a message 'Microsoft Excel cannot find a match'. Click OK to close the message box.
10. Click the Close button to close the Replace dialogue box.
11. Save the spreadsheet.

Hint:

You could use the Replace All button in the Replace dialogue box to replace all the text in one operation. Be cautious. It might replace more than you expect. Suppose that you decided to replace 'her' with 'him'. Smit**her**s would change to Smit**him**s.

Column D contains information on the credit status of the customers. This is confidential information, and it may be appropriate to hide the cells except when specially authorised people are using the spreadsheet.

Method

1 Select cell D1. (Any cell in column D would do.)
2 Click on the Format menu and select Column, then select Hide from the submenu.
3 The width of the column is reduced to zero so that the column disappears. You can see that a column has been hidden because D is missing from the column headings.
4 Cell D1 is still selected. Click on any other cell to deselect cell D1. You could now use the spreadsheet in this form. The credit status is not displayed.
5 To show column D again, you first need to select a cell in it. You cannot do this by clicking with the mouse in the column, because there is nowhere to click. Instead, click into the name box at the left of the formula bar, and key in the cell reference **D1** as shown in Figure 3.10. Press the Enter key.

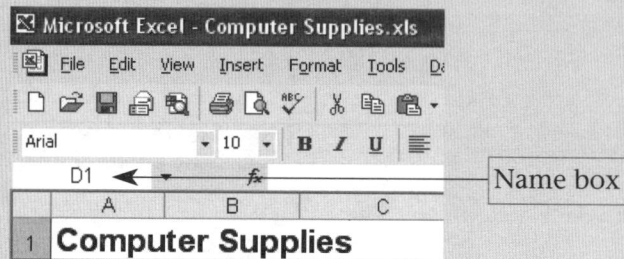

Figure 3.10 The name box

6 The hidden cell D1 should be selected. You should see a dark bar between cells C1 and E1.
7 Click on the Format menu and select Column from the drop down list, then select Unhide from the submenu.
8 Column D should reappear.

Task 3.11 Freeze windows

Freezing windows is used to keep some cells always visible on the screen as the other cells scroll. This is useful for keeping row or column headings on the screen in a large spreadsheet.

In order to demonstrate freezing windows properly, you need a bigger spreadsheet. One option would be to key in another 30 rows of data. You can do this if you wish, inventing new customers and items for them to buy. Alternatively, you can follow the suggested method of copying the existing data several times to make the spreadsheet larger.

Method

1 Select cells A5 to H11 and give the copy command. Click the Copy button or use one of the other methods if you prefer.
2 Select cell A12 and give the paste command.

3 Select cell A19 and paste again. Select A26 and paste. Select A33 and paste. Your spreadsheet should now occupy cells A1 to H39. It is large enough to demonstrate splitting and freezing windows.

4 Use the scrollbar at the right of the spreadsheet to scroll up and down the window. When you scroll down, the column headings of Order date, Customer ID, etc. disappear. This can make it hard to remember what sort of data is in each column.

5 Select cell A4.

6 Click the Window menu and select Freeze Panes from the drop down list.

7 Use the scrollbar to scroll down the spreadsheet. The column headings in row 3 should remain visible.

8 Click the Window menu and select Unfreeze Panes from the drop down list.

9 Use the scrollbar to scroll down the spreadsheet. The headings scroll off the screen as they did originally.

10 Select cell D4.

11 Click the Window menu and select Freeze Panes from the drop down list.

12 The column headings in row 3 should again remain visible as you scroll down. Use the scrollbar at the bottom of the window to scroll to the right. Columns A, B and C should remain visible as the other columns scroll, so that you can still see the customer names.

13 Click the Window menu and select Unfreeze Panes from the drop down list.

Hint:

When you freeze panes, all the columns to the left of your selected cell and all the rows above your selected cell are frozen. They do not scroll. Use freeze panes to keep column and row headings on the screen.

Task 3.12 Split windows

This facility is related to freezing panes, but allows the areas of the window to scroll independently.

Hint:

Use Split Window when you want to look at two areas of your spreadsheet at the same time, but they are too far apart to show in one window.

Method

1 Cell D4 should still be selected.

2 Click the Window menu and select Split.

3 The main area of the spreadsheet is now split into four areas that can be scrolled independently. There are two scrollbars at the right of the window and two scrollbars at the bottom. Use these scrollbars to see how you can scroll each window area.

4 Click the Window menu and select Remove Split.

Task 3.13 Use headers and footers

A header appears at the top of every page. A footer appears at the bottom of every page. They are used to show repeated information such as a title, a name, a date or a page number.

Method

1   Click on the View menu and select Header and Footer from the drop down list. The Page Setup dialogue box appears with the Header/Footer tab in front.

Hint: You could select Page Setup from the File menu and click on the Header/Footer tab in the Page Setup dialogue box. This has the same result as step 1 of the method.

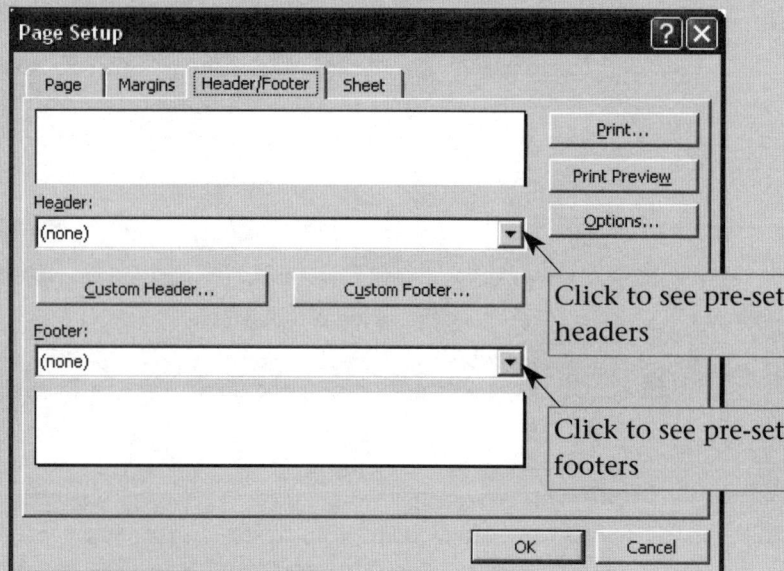

Figure 3.11 Header and Footer section of Page Setup dialogue box

2   Click on the arrow at the right of the box labelled Header. This shows a drop down list of pre-set headers. Options include variations on the page number and the file name. You may wish to use one of these options another time. For now, select None.

3   Excel offers a similar set of options for the footer. Click on the arrow at the right of the box labelled Footer to see the options, then select None. You will be creating your own header and footer.

4   Click on the Custom Footer button. The Footer dialogue box appears.

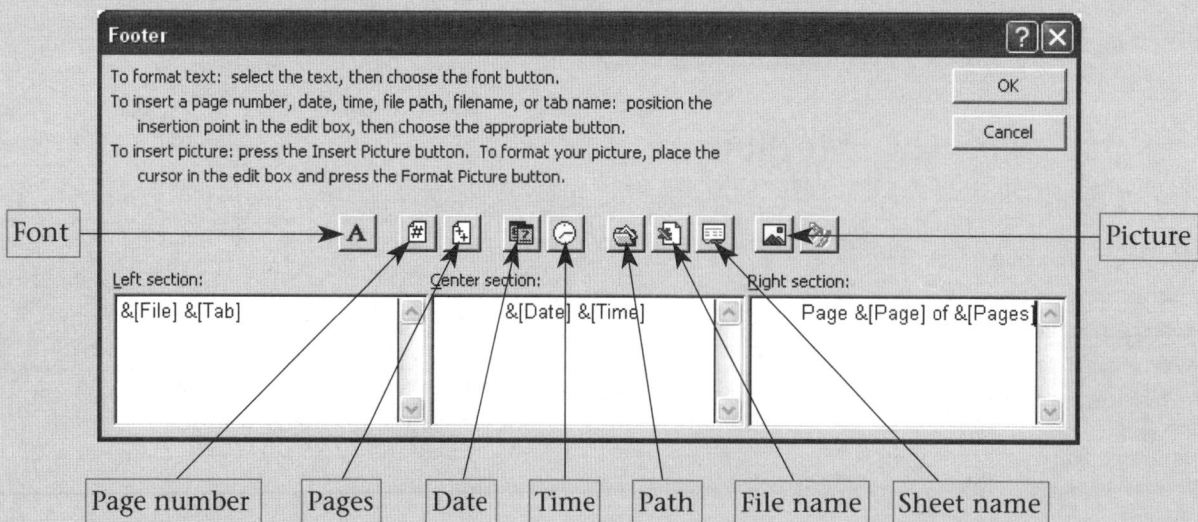

Figure 3.12 The Footer dialogue box

5　The footer is in three sections, left, centre and right. The flashing cursor should be in the left section. Click the File name button, then key in a space, then click the Sheet name button. The codes **&[File] &[Tab]** should appear. These will be replaced with the actual file name and sheet name when the footer is produced. If you want to show the path, you can click the Path button instead of the File Name button.

6　Press the tab key or click into the Centre section. Click the Date button, key in a space, then click the Time button. The codes **&[Date] &[Time]** should appear.

7　Press the tab key or click into the Right section. Key in **Page** followed by a space. Click the Page number button. Key in a space, then key in **of** then another space. Click the Pages button. The right section should now show **Page &[Page] of &[Pages]**.

8　Click OK. The footer box of the Header/Footer dialogue should now show something like **Computer Supplies.xls Sheet 1 25/06/02 17:36 Page 1 of 1**. The date and time should be the current date and time. The text may be squashed or overwritten in the box but it should be all right in the finished footer.

9　Click the Custom Header button. The Header dialogue box should appear. It is similar to the Footer dialogue box.

10　Key in your name in the left section of the header.

11　Select your name by holding down the left mouse button as you move the mouse across the text.

12　Click on the Font button, labelled A. This displays a font dialogue box so that you can choose a different font, style and size for your name. Make your choice, then click OK.

13　Click OK to close the Header dialogue box.

14　Click OK to close the Header/Footer section of the Page Setup dialogue box.

15　Notice that the header and footer do not show on the normal view of the spreadsheet. Click the Print Preview button on the toolbar.

16　You should see that the header and footer appear in the preview.

17　Close the Print Preview without printing by clicking the button labelled Close.

18　Save the spreadsheet.

Hint:

You do not have to use all the available buttons every time you make a header and footer. You have tried out most of them. In future just use what you need.

Task 3.14　Print with/without repeated table headings

If a spreadsheet prints on two or more pages, it can be helpful to repeat headings on the second and later pages.

Method

1　First change to landscape orientation so that all the columns fit on one sheet. To do this, click on the File menu and select Page Setup. Click on the Page tab and select landscape orientation.

2　Click on Print Preview. There should be two pages. The first page shows the title and the column headings. Click the button labelled Next to see the second page. This does not have column headings, so it is not clear what data is in each column.

3　Close the Preview without printing.

4　Click on the File menu and select Page Setup. Click on the Sheet tab in the Page Setup dialogue box.

5　Click into the box labelled 'Rows to repeat at top'.

6　Click in any cell in row 3. You should see **$3:$3** appear in the box. This means row 3. Row 3 contains the headings that must be repeated.

7　Click Print Preview. Now the column headings should be shown on page 2.

8　Print the spreadsheet.

Hint:

If you have a spreadsheet that is more than one page wide and has labelled rows, you can repeat the row labels on every page. In step 5 you would select 'Columns to repeat at left'. You would then click into the column containing the row labels and preview as before.

By default, gridlines, column letters and row numbers are shown on the screen but they are not printed. You can choose to print them.

Method

1   Click on the File menu and select Page Setup. Click on the Sheet tab in the Page Setup dialogue box.
2   Click in the check boxes labelled 'Gridlines' and 'Row and column headings' to place ticks. Click OK.
3   Print preview. Gridlines, column letters and row numbers should be shown. It is not necessary to print again, but you could do so if you like.
4   Save the spreadsheet and close it. Close down Excel.

Remember:

Take regular breaks. This could be a good time to take a break.

→ Practise your skills 3.1: Salads spreadsheet

You will create a spreadsheet to find the profit on sales of salads. If you cannot remember the methods, look back at the tasks earlier in this section.

1   Load Excel if it is not already open.

2   Create a new spreadsheet as shown in Figure 3.13.

	A	B	C	D	E	F	G	H	I
1	**Salads**		Date	12/09/2002					
2									
3	Item	No in crate	No of crates	Price of crate	Cost to buy	No bought	No sold	Selling price	Takings
4	Lettuces - round	12	6	£ 5.00			61	£ 0.42	
5	Lettuces - cos	12	6	£ 5.50			65	£ 0.85	
6	Lettuces - iceberg	8	8	£ 6.00			64	£ 0.99	

Figure 3.13 Salads spreadsheet

3   Save the spreadsheet as **Salad.xls.**

4   In cell E4, enter a formula to multiply the number of crates by the price of a crate.

5   In cell F4, enter a formula to multiply the number of lettuces in a crate by the number of crates.

6   Replicate both these formulas down to rows 5 and 6.

7   In cell I4, enter a formula to multiply the number sold by the selling price.

8   Replicate this formula down to rows 5 and 6.

9   Starting in cell A20, enter additional data.

	A	B	C	D	E	F	G	H	I
20	Peppers - green	20	3	£ 2.00			48	£ 0.20	
21	Peppers - red	20	3	£ 2.20			41	£ 0.22	
22	Peppers - yellow	20	2	£ 2.20			40	£ 0.22	

Figure 3.14 Peppers for the spreadsheet

10   Copy the formulas from cells E4 to F6 and paste them into cells E20 to F22.

11   Copy the formulas from cells I4 to I6 and paste them to cells I20 to I22.

12   Go to cell A10 and split the window. Scroll down the lower part of the window to cell 40.   →

13 Enter additional data starting in row 40.

40	Tomato - standard	100	3	£	8.00			281	£	0.15
41	Tomato - cherry	200	2	£	16.00			295	£	0.08
42	Tomato - beef	50	3	£	10.00			138	£	0.25

Figure 3.15 Tomatoes for the spreadsheet

14 Copy formulas from the lettuce entries as before. You should be able to see the lettuce entries and the tomato entries on the screen at the same time.

15 Remove the split window.

16 Starting in row 44, create a summary section of the spreadsheet to find the profit. The summary section should look like Figure 3.16. Some of the cells contain formulas as follows:

- Cell E44 contains =**SUM(E4:E42)**
- Cell I44 contains =**SUM(I4:I42)** (Note letter I, not number 1.)
- Cell E46 contains =**I44-E44**
- Cell E48 contains =**E46-E47**

	A	B	C	D	E	F	G	H	I
44				Totals	£ 214.00				£ 271.90
45									
46				Gross profit	£ 57.90				
47			Overheads and expenses	£ 25.00					
48				Net profit	£ 32.90				

Figure 3.16 Summary section of the spreadsheet

17 Save the spreadsheet.

18 Put your name in a header. Put the date, the file name and the page number in a footer.

19 Go to column B and insert a new column.

20 In the new cell B3, key in a heading: **Supplier**.

21 Enter supplier names. The lettuces all come from MacArthur Growers. The peppers come from ABC Imports. The tomatoes come from Guernsey Tomatoes.

22 Print the spreadsheet in landscape orientation. Show gridlines, row numbers and column letters. Also show the headings in row 3 on each page. There should be two pages.

23 Save the spreadsheet again.

24 Save a second copy of the spreadsheet as **Salads2.xls**. Work on Salads2.xls from now on.

25 Use Find and Replace to change ABC Imports to **Southern Produce** each time it occurs.

26 Insert a new row above the existing row 6. Move the data for round lettuces to this new row. Delete the empty row 4.

27 Hide rows 7 to 19. Hide rows 23 to 39. Hide columns G, H and I.

28 Print the spreadsheet again. Save and close the spreadsheet.

→ Check your knowledge

1 Cell A3 contains the number 32. You use the fill handle to fill down to cell A6. What will be in cell A6?

2 Cell B3 contains the number 32. You hold down the Ctrl key as you use the fill handle to fill down to cell B6. What will be in cell B6?

3 Cell C3 contains the text **Monday**. You use the fill handle to fill down to cell C6. What will be in cell C6?

4 Cell D3 contains the text **Alison**. You use the fill handle to fill down to cell D6. What will be in cell D6?

5 You point the mouse to the centre of a spreadsheet cell. What does the mouse pointer look like?

6 You point the mouse to the border of a spreadsheet cell. What does the mouse pointer look like?

7 You point the mouse to the fill handle of a spreadsheet cell. What does the mouse pointer look like?

8 Drag and drop normally moves cell contents. Which keyboard key do you press to copy cell contents using drag and drop?

9 What is the difference between splitting the window and freezing panes?

10 You need to see cell K42 and cell Z97 on the screen at the same time. Would you split the window or freeze panes?

You will learn to

- Use the SUM, AVERAGE, MAX and MIN functions
- Use the COUNT, ROUND and DATE functions
- Print a spreadsheet showing formulas
- Hide formulas in a printout
- Use relative and absolute references
- Use named ranges
- Use an IF function
- Use relational operators
- Choose data for testing formulas
- Test and correct formulas

Information: Using formulas and functions

Formulas

Spreadsheets must give the right results. This means that the input data must be right and the formulas must be right. It is easy to make a keying in error in a formula so that it does the wrong calculation. All formulas should therefore be checked. The more complicated the formula, the more checking is likely to be needed. In this section you will be using plenty of formulas and checking that they give the right results.

You should already know how to use the four arithmetic operators +, −, * and / in formulas. You should also know how to combine them, using brackets where necessary. Excel uses the normal rules for carrying out calculations in order. Brackets come first, then multiply and divide, then add and subtract. For example,

$= 4 + 6 * 2$ gives 16 because the multiplying is done first.
$= (4 + 6) * 2$ gives 20 because the brackets are worked out first.

Functions

A function takes in data, processes it, and produces a result. The name of the function shows the kind of processing that is carried out. Every function name is followed by round brackets. Input data for the function goes in the brackets. You can use functions in formulas to carry out special calculations.

The most common function is the SUM function. This adds up whatever it finds in its brackets. Often there is a range of cells in the brackets, e.g. SUM(B4:B8). There can be several ranges of cells, or individual cells or values in the brackets, separated by commas, e.g. SUM(B4:B8, E5:E7, F7, G7, 250). There can even be other calculations inside the brackets, e.g. SUM(C1*C2, D1*D2, E1*E2). This last function would multiply C1 by C2, D1 by D2 and E1 by E2, then add up the →

> **Hint:**
>
> One way of remembering the order of carrying out arithmetic operations is to say BODMAS to yourself. Brackets, Of, Divide, Multiply, Add, Subtract.

answers. Remember that SUM is for adding. Do not use it if you just want to multiply, divide or subtract.

You may have met the AVERAGE, MAX and MIN functions at Level 1. The AVERAGE function takes the range of cells or values in its brackets and finds the average value. MAX finds the maximum (highest) value. MIN finds the minimum (lowest) value.

The COUNT function takes the range of cells in its brackets and finds how many of those cells contain number entries. It does not count empty cells or cells with text entries. It does count cells that contain formulas with a number result.

There are several functions for handling dates and times. Two useful date functions are TODAY which finds today's date from the computer's system clock and displays it, and NOW which finds the date and the time. Both these functions have empty brackets because they do not need to take in data from other cells.

The ROUND function is used for rounding a value to a chosen number of decimal places. It needs two items of data in its brackets. First, it needs the value to be rounded, or a reference or formula that gives the value. Second, it needs to be told how many decimal places to use. For example,

= ROUND(12.383, 2) would give 12.38.
= ROUND(12.383, 1) would give 12.4.

Task 4.1   Use the SUM, AVERAGE, MAX and MIN functions

You will create a spreadsheet to show a company's exports to four countries over a four year period. The exports are given in millions of pounds.

Method

I   Create a new spreadsheet as shown in Figure 4.1. Save it as **Exports.xls.**

	A	B	C	D	E
1	**Exports**				
2					
3	Millions of pounds				
4					
5	**Country**	**Year 1**	**Year 2**	**Year 3**	**Year 4**
6	**USA**	12.4	14.3	13.7	16.2
7	**Canada**	9.7	10.5	9.4	9.8
8	**Germany**	15.1	15.8	16.1	16.9
9	**France**	6.2	7.8	12.3	10.5
10					
11	**Total for year**				
12	**Average for year**				
13	**Maximum**				
14	**Minimum**				

Figure 4.1 The Exports spreadsheet

2. In cell B11, put in the formula =**SUM(B6:B9)** to find the total exports for Year 1. The result should be 43.4.

3. In cell B12, put in the formula =**AVERAGE(B6:B9)** to find the average exports per country for Year 1. The result should be 10.85.

4. In cell B13, put in the formula =**MAX(B6:B9)** to find the maximum exports to any country for Year 1. The result should be 15.1.

5. In cell B14, put in the formula =**MIN(B6:B9)** to find the minimum exports to any country for Year 1. The result should be 6.2.

6. Select cells B11 to B14. Use the fill handle in the lower right corner of the selection to copy the formulas across to columns C, D and E.

Task 4.2	Use the COUNT, ROUND and DATE functions

Method

1. In cell B16, put in the formula =**COUNT(B6:B9)** to count the number of entries in the cells. The result should be 4.

2. Use the fill handle to copy the formula from cell B16 to cells C16, D16 and E16.

3. The COUNT function can be useful for checking that there are no missing entries. Delete the entry from cell B7. The result of the count for column B should change to 3. Key in the entry of 9.7 into cell B7 again. The count should go back to 4.

4. The average in cell B12 is shown as 10.85. Use the Formatting toolbar or the Format menu to format cell B12 to display 1 decimal place. B12 should display 10.9.

5. Although B12 displays 10.9, it still holds the value of 10.85. To show this, go to cell B18 and enter the formula =**B12*10**. The result is 108.5, showing that B12 still holds 10.85.

6. Format B12 to show 2 decimal places so that 10.85 is displayed in the cell again.

7. Change the formula in B12 to =**ROUND(AVERAGE(B6:B9),1)**. Take care with the brackets. You are using the ROUND function to take the result of the AVERAGE function and round it to 1 decimal place.

8. Check that cell B12 displays 10.90. Cell B18 should now display 109. Formatting just changes the display and does not affect the number held in the cell. The ROUND function does change the number that is held in the cell and used for calculations.

9. Use the fill handle to copy the formula from cell B12 to C12, D12 and E12.

10. Format the four cells to display 1 decimal place.

11. Delete the test formula from cell B18.

12. In cell E1 put the formula =**TODAY()**. Do not leave out the brackets. They are needed, even though they are empty, to show that TODAY is a function.

13. The date should appear in the cell. It should be formatted correctly as a date. If not, you can change the format yourself.

14. Save your spreadsheet now.

Task 4.3 — Print a spreadsheet showing formulas

Method

1   Display the formulas as you learned for Level 1. You can select Options from the Tools menu and click the Formulas check box. Alternatively you can hold down the Ctrl key and press the 'Start quote and lines' key on the keyboard.

Figure 4.2 Shortcut key to show formulas

2   The formulas need to be shown in full. Make cells wider if necessary.
3   Change to landscape orientation. (File menu, Page Setup.)
4   Preview and print.

Task 4.4 — Hide formulas in a printout

You can hide your formulas if you do not want other people to see how your spreadsheet works. You will hide some of the formulas as a demonstration of this method.

Hint:

Always save before switching to formula view. You may need to change column widths in formula view but you do not want these changes saved. Close without saving again. Your spreadsheet will stay as it was when you last saved it. Alternatively, you can use the Undo button on the toolbar to restore columns to their original widths.

Method

1   Select cells B11 to C16.
2   Click on the Format menu and select Cells from the drop down list. Click on the Protection tab.
3   Click in the Hidden check box to place a tick. Click OK.
4   Click on the Tools menu and select Protection from the drop down list. Choose Protect Sheet from the submenu. Do not use a password. Click OK.
5   Formulas are not displayed in the hidden cells. Cells that are not hidden show formulas as usual.
6   Preview and print again. Write 'hidden formulas' on the printout.
7   Switch back from formula view to the normal results view. Results are displayed in the hidden cells, but there is no formula shown in the formula bar when you select a hidden cell.
8   Close the spreadsheet without saving it again.

Information: Relative and absolute references

The topic of relative and absolute references was introduced at Level 1. Here we revisit the topic in more detail.

Normally cell references are relative. When you use a cell reference in a formula, Excel treats the position of the cell as relative to the position of the formula. For example, suppose you go to cell A3 and enter the formula **=A1*A2**. Excel treats this as meaning 'two-cells-up-from-here multiplied by one-cell-up-from-here'. Suppose you then copy the formula to cell D7. The formula becomes **=D5*D6**. It still means 'two-cells-up-from-here multiplied by one-cell-up-from-here'. Most of the time you will want formulas to behave like this when they are copied.

Sometimes you may want to refer to a particular cell in a formula, and not let the reference change when the formula is copied. You need an absolute reference. An absolute reference is shown by dollar signs. Suppose the formula in cell A3 was **=$A$1*A2**. When you copy this formula to cell D7 it becomes **=$A$1*D6**. The reference to cell A1 is absolute and does not change on copying. The reference to cell A2 is relative, and it changes on copying.

You can have a mixed reference, partly absolute and partly relative. The dollar sign fixes the column letter or row number immediately after it. You can fix the column but let the row change. In the formula **=$A1*A2**, the reference **$A1** is mixed. The column letter A is absolute but the row number 1 is relative and can change. When you copy this formula to cell D7 it becomes **=$A5*D6**. You can fix the row but let the column change. In the formula **=A$1*A2**, the reference **A$1** is mixed. The column letter A is relative and can change but the row number 1 is absolute. When you copy this formula to cell D7 it becomes **=D$1*D6**.

This may seem complicated at first. The next few tasks give you practice in using relative, absolute and mixed references and they should help to make it clear.

Task 4.5 — Use an absolute reference

You will create a spreadsheet to work out the takings from several car boot sales after paying for the pitch.

Method

I   Create a new spreadsheet and enter data as shown in Figure 4.3.

	A	B	C	D
1	**Car Boot Sales**			
2				
3	**Takings before paying for pitch**			
4		April	May	June
5	Meadow Farm	32.56	47.87	43.21
6	Long Acre	28.45	10.21	30.98
7	Playing field	68.77	53.33	63.25
8				
9	**Pitch cost**	£ 7.50		
10				
11	**Takings after paying for pitch**			
12		April	May	June
13	Meadow Farm			
14	Long Acre			
15	Playing field			

Figure 4.3 The Boot sales spreadsheet

2 Go to cell B13 and enter the formula **=B5-$B$9**.

You could key this formula in or you could enter it as follows:

- Key in =
- Click in cell B5
- Key in −
- Click in cell B9
- Press the F4 function key on the keyboard to convert B9 to an absolute reference $B$9.

3 Use the fill handle to copy the formula from cell B13 to cells B14 and B15.

4 Select cells B13 to B15 and use the fill handle to copy across to columns C and D.

5 Check the results. £7.50 should have been subtracted from each original takings value. Look at the formulas in the cells to see how the absolute reference has worked.

6 Save the spreadsheet as **Boot sales.xls.**

7 Print the spreadsheet and the formulas if you wish. Close the spreadsheet.

| Task 4.6 | Use a mixed reference and fill down |

You will create a ready reckoner to convert euros to pounds.

Method

I Create a new spreadsheet and enter data as shown in Figure 4.4.

	A	B
1	**Euros to Pounds**	
2	**Ready reckoner**	
3		
4	**Conversion rate**	0.612
5		
6	**Euros**	**Pounds**
7	1	
8	2	
9	3	
10	4	
11	5	
12	6	
13	7	
14	8	
15	9	
16	10	

Figure 4.4 The Euros spreadsheet

2 Go to cell B7 and enter the formula **=A7*$B$4**.

3 Use the fill handle to copy the formula down the column to cell B16.

4 Save the spreadsheet as **Euros.xls.**

5 The absolute reference **$B$4** works correctly and you could leave the spreadsheet as it is. The purpose of this task is to show you how to use a mixed reference, so we will continue and make some changes.

6 When you copy the formula, you copy to different rows, but keep the column the same. There is no need to fix the column letter in the reference because it would not change anyway. Only the row needs to be fixed. Go back to cell B7 and change the formula to **=A7*B$4**.

7 Use the fill handle to copy the new formula down the column to cell B16.

8 The results should be the same as before.

9 Save the spreadsheet again.

10 Print if you wish, then close the spreadsheet.

Task 4.7   Use a mixed reference and fill across

You will create a spreadsheet to work out scores in a quiz. There is a special bonus round where the scores are multiplied by a magic number to give a bonus which is added to the score. The leading team chooses the magic number, which can be 2, 3 or 4, before the start of the bonus round.

Method

1 Create a new spreadsheet and enter data as shown in Figure 4.5.

	A	B	C	D	E
1	**Bonus Quiz**				
2					
3	**Chosen magic number**	**3**			
4					
5		**Team 1**	**Team 2**	**Team 3**	**Team 4**
6	Round 1	8	5	10	7
7	Round 2	7	6	8	8
8	Round 3	5	7	4	5
9	Bonus for Round 3				
10	Round 4	8	4	9	8
11	**Total score**				

Figure 4.5 Bonus quiz spreadsheet

2 Go to cell B9 and enter a formula to multiply the score for Round 3 by the magic number to give the bonus. You could use **=B8*$B$3**. This formula would give the correct results when it is copied to cells C9, D9 and E9. You are learning about mixed references, so use **=B8*$B3** instead. This fixes the column so that the reference will not change from B3 to C3, D3 or E3. The row does not need to be fixed. You are filling along a row, so the row number in the reference would not change anyway.

3 Replicate the formula from B9 along the row to C9, D9 and E9. Check the formula in each cell to make sure that each score is multiplied by the magic number in B3.

When you enter a cell reference into a formula you can press the F4 function key to make the reference absolute. If you press F4 a second time, you fix only the row. If you press F4 a third time, you fix only the column. If you press F4 a fourth time, the whole reference becomes relative again.

4 Go to cell B11 and enter a formula to find the total score for Team 1. Replicate this formula to find the totals for the other teams.

5 Check the calculations. There should be a dead heat with each team scoring a total of 43.

6 Save the spreadsheet as **Bonus quiz.xls**.

7 Print if you wish. Close the spreadsheet.

Task 4.8   Fill mixed references down and across

This is the ultimate challenge in using mixed references. You will create a set of times tables by keying in only one formula and copying it. You are unlikely ever to have to use references as complicated as this again, but challenge yourself. If you understand this task then you know that you fully understand relative, absolute and mixed references.

Method

1 Create a new spreadsheet and enter data as shown in Figure 4.6. Make full use of the fill handle and the Ctrl key.

	A	B	C	D	E	F	G	H	I	J	K
1	Times tables										
2											
3			1	2	3	4	5	6	7	8	9	10
4	1										
5	2										
6	3										
7	4										
8	5										
9	6										
10	7										
11	8										
12	9										
13	10										

Figure 4.6 Times tables spreadsheet

2 The next step is to enter a formula into cell B4. This formula must be chosen so that you can copy it along the rows and down the column to fill up the times table grid, giving the right answers.
Start with the basic formula: **=A4*B3**. As you copy this along the row, the column numbers will change to **=B4*C3**, **=C4*D3**, etc. This is not what you want. Try it out and see.

3 You want to multiply by A4 each time, but allow the second cell to change. The cell reference A4 needs to have its column fixed by using **$A4**.
The second attempt at a formula is **=$A4*B3**. This would work perfectly when copied along row 4. Try it out. Unfortunately it does not work when you copy it down to other rows.

4   As you copy from B4 down to B5 and B6 and beyond, the formula changes to **=$A5*B4**, **=$A6*B5**, and so on. You want to multiply by B3 every time and not let the row number change in the second cell reference. The cell reference B3 needs to have its row number fixed by using B$3.

5   The third attempt at a formula is **=$A4*B$3**. Enter this formula in cell B4.

6   Replicate the formula along the row to cell K4.

7   Select cells B4 to K4 and replicate down to row 13.

8   Check that your table is complete and giving the right answers.

9   Save the spreadsheet as **Times tables.xls.**

10   Print if you wish. Close the spreadsheet.

Information: Named ranges

You can give a name to a single cell or to a range of cells. Names can be used in formulas instead of cell references. This can help to make formulas easier to read and understand. It can also help you to avoid any problems with absolute references because a reference to a named cell or range is always absolute.

Task 4.9 Use a named cell

You will make a second version of your Boot sales spreadsheet that uses a named cell in formulas instead of an absolute reference.

Method

1   Open your Boot sales spreadsheet and save a copy of it as **Boot sales2.xls.** Work with Boot sales2 from now on.

2   Select cell B9, the cell containing the pitch cost.

3   Click on the Insert menu and select Name, then select Define from the submenu. The Define Name dialogue box opens.

4   The box offers you the name Pitch_cost, taken from the label in the cell on the left. Spaces are not allowed in names, so it puts in the underline character instead of the space. You could keep this name, but it may be easier to use a simpler name. Key in **Pitch** to replace Pitch_cost. Click the button labelled Add.

5   The name is copied into the main list area of the dialogue box. Click OK.

6   Delete the formulas from cells B13 to D15.

7   Go to cell B13 and enter the formula **=B5-Pitch**.

8   Copy the formula across to cells C13 and D13, then copy all three cells down to rows 14 and 15.

9   The results should be exactly the same as they were before. You have used a named cell in the formula instead of using an absolute reference to cell B9.

10   Save the spreadsheet and close it.

You will make a second version of your Bonus quiz spreadsheet that uses a named cell and named ranges of cells in formulas.

Method

1 Open your Bonus quiz spreadsheet and save a copy of it as **Bonus quiz2.xls.**

2 Select cell B3, the cell containing the magic number.

3 Click on the Insert menu and select Name, then select Define from the submenu. Enter the name **magic** into the Define Name dialogue box. Click Add, then click OK.

4 Select the range of cells B6 to B10. Using the same method as step 3, give the range of cells the name **Team1**. Do not leave a space.

5 Select cells C6 to C10 and give them the name **Team2**.

6 Select cells D6 to D10 and give them the name **Team3**.

7 Select cells E6 to E10 and give them the name **Team4**. You should now have five named ranges in the list in the Define Name dialogue box.

8 Delete the formulas in cells B9 to E9.

9 Go to cell B9 and enter the formula **=B8*magic.**

10 Replicate the formula across to cells C9, D9 and E9. The results should be the same as before.

11 Delete the formulas in cells B11 to E11.

12 Go to cell B11 and enter the formula **=SUM(Team1)**. You should be able to do this by using the Autosum button on the toolbar.

13 Enter similar formulas in cells C11, D11 and E11 to find the totals for the other teams. You have to enter these formulas separately. You cannot copy from cell B11 because you would be finding the total for team 1 every time.

14 Save the spreadsheet and close it.

Information: IF functions and relational operators

If you choose the number 15 then you win the prize, otherwise you do not.
If you spend more than £50 then postage and packing is free, otherwise you pay £5.
If you have £1000 or more in your savings account then the interest rate is 4%, otherwise it is 3.5%.

These **IF statements** can all be split into the same parts.

- If
- A statement or condition that can be true or false, e.g. 'you spend more than £50'.
- Then
- Something that happens if the statement is true, e.g. 'postage and packing is free'.
- Otherwise
- Something that happens if the statement is false, e.g. 'you pay £5'.

Excel provides an IF function that follows this pattern. It uses commas in place of the words 'then' and 'otherwise'.

→

If you choose the number 15 then you win the prize, otherwise you do not.
Suppose that cell B2 contains the number that you have chosen.

Cell C2 tells you whether you have won or not. It contains the formula:

=IF(B2=15, "you win","you lose")

Read this example as 'If cell B2 = 15 then show "you win" in this cell, otherwise show "you lose" in this cell'.

The condition that can be true or false is B2=15. The first comma in the brackets means then. The second comma means otherwise. The values to go in the cell have double quotes since they are text data. Numbers would not have quotes.

If you spend more than £50 then postage and packing is free, otherwise you pay £5.
Suppose that the amount you spend is in cell B11.
The postage and packing cell contains the formula:

=IF(B11>50,0,5)

Read this example as 'If cell B11 is greater than 50 then show 0 in this cell, otherwise show 5 in this cell'.

If you spend more than £50 then the postage and packing cell will show 0, otherwise it will show 5.

If you have £1000 or more in your savings account then the interest rate is 4%, otherwise it is 3.5%.
Suppose that cell B9 shows the amount in your savings account.
Cell C9 shows the interest rate. It contains the formula:

=IF(B9>=1000,4%,3.5%)

Read this example as 'If cell B9 is greater than or equal to 1000 then show 4% in this cell, otherwise show 3.5% in this cell'.

If you have £1000 or more then the interest rate cell will show as 4%, otherwise it will show as 3.5%.

The IF function is rather different from the formulas and functions you have met before, but you will have plenty of practice so that you will get used to using it.

Task 4.11   Use an IF function

Method

1   Create a new spreadsheet like Figure 4.7. Save it with the name **If demo.xls**.

	A	B
1	**IF demonstration**	
2	Enter a number	4
3		

Figure 4.7 IF demonstration spreadsheet

2   In cell C2, key in the formula **=IF(B2=15, "you win","you lose")** and press Enter.

3   Cell B2 does not contain 15. The condition **B2=15** is false. The 'otherwise' part of the IF function is "you lose", so this appears in the cell containing the function.

4 Go to cell B2 and change its contents to 15. Now the condition **B2=15** is true. The 'then' part of the IF function is "you win" so this appears in the cell containing the function.

5 Change cell B2 to other values. 15 is the only value that makes the condition true and makes "you win" appear.

Information: Relational operators

The relational operators are:

=   equals
>   greater than
<   less than
>= greater than or equal to
<= less than or equal to
<> not equal to

You can use any of these in the condition part of an IF function.

Task 4.12 | Use relational operators

Method

1 Make additional entries in your If demo spreadsheet as shown in Figure 4.8.

4	Enter a number less than 20	10	=IF(B4<20,"Good","Too big")
5	Enter a number, 20 or less	10	=IF(B5<=20,"Good","Too big")
6	Enter a number more than 5	10	=IF(B6>5,"Good","Too small")
7	Enter a number, 5 or more	10	=IF(B7>=5,"Good","Too small")
8			
9	Interest rate	10	=IF(B9>=1000, 4%, 3.5%)
10			
11	Postage and packing	10	=IF(B11>50, 0, 5)
12			
13	Enter your name		=IF(B13="","Name not there","")

Figure 4.8 More entries for the If demo spreadsheet

2 Cell B4 contains 10, so the condition **B4<20** is true. The formula in cell C4 should give the result **Good**.

3 Change the number in cell B4 to 30. The condition **B4<20** is now false, so cell C4 should show **Too big**.

4 Decide what will happen if you change B4 to 20. Try it out.

5 Cell B5 contains 10, so the condition **B5<=20** is true. The formula in cell C5 should give the result **Good**.

6 Change the number in cell B5 to 30. The condition **B5<=20** is now false, so cell C5 should show **Too big**.

7 Decide what will happen if you change B5 to 20. Try it out. This demonstrates the difference between greater than (>) and greater than or equal to (>=).

8   Cell B6 contains 10 so the condition **B6>5** is true. The formula in cell C6 should give the result **Good**.

9   Change the number in cell B6 to 2. The condition **B6>5** is now false, so cell C6 should show **Too small**.

10 Cell B7 contains 10 so the condition **B7>=5** is true. The formula in cell C7 should give the result **Good**.

11 Change the number in cell B7 to 2. The condition **B7>=5** is now false, so cell C7 should show **Too small**.

12 What happens if you put the value 5 in cells B6 and B7? Decide what will happen first and then try it out.

Here are the remaining two examples that we started with in the information section (pages 48–49).

13 Cell B9 contains 10 so the condition **B9>=1000** is false. The formula in cell C9 should give the result 0.035. Format the cell as percent and it will show 3.5%.

14 Change the number in cell B9 to 2000. The condition **B9>=1000** is now true, so cell C9 should show 4%.

15 Cell B11 contains 10 so the condition **B11>50** is false. The formula in cell C11 should give the result 5.

16 Change the number in cell B11 to 100. The condition **B11>50** is now true so cell C11 should show 0.

Finally, there is an example that uses text in the condition as well as in the results. Text is enclosed in double quotes. If there is a pair of double quotes with nothing between them then it means that there is no text. The cell is empty.

17 Cell B13 is empty. The condition **B13=""** is true. Cell C13 should display the text **Name not there**. If it does not then check the formula carefully to make sure that you have the double quotes entered correctly. You need to use the double quote symbol on the 2 key. Two single quotes will not do. There must not be a space between the double quotes. The commas need to be in exactly the right place. The formula should be: **=IF(B13="","Name not there","")**

18 Enter your name in cell B13. The condition **B13=""** is now false. Cell C13 should show nothing.

Information: Choosing data for testing formulas

Before moving on, we will consider how spreadsheet formulas should be tested, and then test the formulas on the IF demonstration spreadsheet in more detail.

Spreadsheets are often designed to be reused many times. They can contain many formulas and some of the formulas can be complicated. These formulas must be tested before the spreadsheet goes into use. To test a formula, you carry out the calculation yourself, either in your head if it is easy, on paper, or using a pocket calculator. You compare your own result with the result of the formula. →

You should test formulas several times, using different numbers as input data. Start with **representative** data: the sort of numbers you would expect the spreadsheet user to enter. You can choose easy numbers to make your own calculations easy. The numbers 10 and 30 that you used when testing the IF functions are representative data.

You should test formulas using **marginal** data. This applies to formulas such as ones with IF functions where there is a marginal value. At the marginal value the result changes. The IF function in cell C4 has the condition **B4<20**. You should test using the number 20 because it is at the margin where the formula result changes from Good to Too big. You should also test using a number just the other side of the margin, so you need a number just less than 20. If you are only interested in whole numbers then choose 19. If numbers with fractional parts are important then go a bit closer to 20, with 19.9, 19.99, etc. Also use a number just the other side of 20, such as 21 or 20.1, 20.01, etc.

Test formulas with **extreme** data. Try very big numbers, very small numbers, zero, maybe negative numbers that are at the extreme limits of what is acceptable.

Test formulas with **rogue** data. This is data that is not acceptable. You might try entering text where a number is expected.

Task 4.13	Test formulas in the demonstration spreadsheet

Method

1   Test the formula in cell C6 by entering test data in cell B6. You need to work out for yourself what the result should be so that you can see if the formula's result is correct.
   - Representative (normal) values: 10, 2.
   - Marginal values: 5, 6, 4, 5.01, 4.99.
   - Extreme values: 100000, 0, −100000.
   - Rogue values: enter some text. Does Excel give you an error message?

2   Look at the formulas in cells C7, C9 and C11. Decide on suitable test data and test the formulas. Take particular care in choosing the marginal values for each formula.

3   Save the spreadsheet again and close it.

Task 4.14 — Use IF functions in an invoice spreadsheet

You will set up a spreadsheet to find the cost of clothes bought by mail order. Prices do not include VAT so this must be added where appropriate. Purchases over £100 have a discount.

Method

1   Create a new spreadsheet as shown in Figure 4.9. Save it with the name **Mail Order Clothes.xls**.

	A	B	C	D	E	F	G	H
1	**Mail Order Clothes**							
2								
3	Cat No	Item	Code	Unit Price	Number	Cost	VAT	Cost with VAT
4	D132	Dress size 14	A	£ 32.99	1			
5	F548	Child's shorts	C	£ 20.50	2			
6	C202	T shirt - large	A	£ 14.99	2			
7	F593	Child's T shirt	C	£ 12.50	1			
8								
9	Code: A for adult, C for child						Subtotal	
10	£5 discount on orders over £100.						Discount	
11							Total	

Figure 4.9 Mail Order Clothes spreadsheet

2   In cell F4, enter a formula to multiply the unit price by the number of items purchased. Replicate (copy) this formula down to cells F5, F6 and F7.

3   In cell G4 you will enter a formula that will show VAT at 17.5% for adult clothes but no VAT for children's clothes. You use the code that shows A for adult or C for child. The formula should contain an IF function to do the following: If the code is "A" then display the cost multiplied by 17.5% otherwise display 0. Try to enter this formula yourself. If you get stuck, you will find the answer at the end of the method.

4   Replicate the formula from cell G4 down to cells G5, G6 and G7.

5   In cell H4 enter a formula to find the cost including VAT. Replicate this formula down to cells H5, H6, H7 and H8.

6   In cell H9, enter a formula to find the subtotal.

7   In cell H10, enter a formula with an IF function. If the subtotal is greater than 100, then the discount is 5, otherwise the discount is 0.

8   In cell H11, enter a formula to subtract the discount from the subtotal to give the final total to be paid.

9   Put your name in a header. Put the date and the file name in a footer.

10   Format all cells containing amounts of money to currency with 2 decimal places. Apply any other formatting you need. Unlock the data entry cells and protect the spreadsheet.

11   Save the spreadsheet.

12   Print the spreadsheet on one sheet of paper. Write printout 1 on the sheet. Check the calculations yourself using a pocket calculator to make sure that your own results agree with the results from the formulas. The subtotal should be £127.49, the discount £5 and the final total £122.49.

13   Delete the data in cells A5 to E5.

14   Enter new data in cells A5 to E5. The new order is: Cat No **C887**, Item **Socks**, Code **A**, Unit price **£3.99**, Number 1.

15   Row 5 should now have £0.70 VAT added. There should now be no discount, and the final total should be £91.18.

16 Save the spreadsheet again.

17 Print the spreadsheet. Write Printout 2 on the sheet.

18 Print the spreadsheet showing formulas, showing gridlines and showing row and column headings. Write Printout 3 on the sheet.

The formulas should be as shown in Figure 4.10.

The formula in cell G4 is: **=IF(C4="A",F4*17.5%,0)**

The formula in cell H10 is: **=IF(H9>100,5,0)**

	A	B	C	D	E	F	G	H
1	Mail Order Clothes							
2								
3	Cat No	Item	Code	Unit Price	Number	Cost	VAT	Cost with VAT
4	D132	Dress size 14	A	32.99	1	=D4*E4	=IF(C4="A",F4*17.5%,0)	=F4+G4
5	C887	Socks	A	3.99	1	=D5*E5	=IF(C5="A",F5*17.5%,0)	=F5+G5
6	C202	T shirt - large	A	14.99	2	=D6*E6	=IF(C6="A",F6*17.5%,0)	=F6+G6
7	F593	Child's T shirt	C	12.5	1	=D7*E7	=IF(C7="A",F7*17.5%,0)	=F7+G7
8								
9	Code: A for adult, C for child						Subtotal	=SUM(H4:H7)
10	£5 discount on orders over £100.						Discount	=IF(H9>100,5,0)
11							Total	=H9-H10

Figure 4.10 Formulas for Mail Order Clothes

Task 4.15 Test and correct formulas

You will create a new spreadsheet and test it. There are some mistakes in the formulas that you are asked to key in. Key them in exactly as given. You will have a chance to correct them later.

Method

1 Create a new spreadsheet as shown in Figure 4.11. Save it with the name **Gifts.xls.**

	A	B	C	D	E
1	Gift Catalogue				
2					
3	Code	Item description	Unit price	Number	Cost
4	GH234	Greetings card pack	£ 5.50	4	=C4+D4
5	FK43	Calendar	£ 1.20	3	=C5+D5
6	FK56	Pen with initials	£ 4.30	2	=C6+D6
7	KL55	Bath robe with initials	£ 18.00	2	=C7+D7
8					
9				Subtotal	=SUM(E4:E8)
10	Carriage £5 on orders under £50			Carriage	=IF(E9>50,5,0)
11				Total	=SUM(E4:E10)

Figure 4.11 The Gift spreadsheet

2 Test the formulas. You can change any of the numbers in cells C4 to D7 as you test. Correct any mistakes you find in the formulas. You should find that the final total is £70.20 using the input data as given when all the mistakes are corrected.

3 Save the spreadsheet when you are happy that all the formulas are correct. Do this before reading on.

4 Here are the corrections:
- Cell E4 should have the formula =C4*D4. The values should be multiplied, not added.
- Cells E5, E6 and E7 should also multiply, not add.
- The condition in the IF function in cell E10 is wrong. It should be E9<50, so the full formula should be =IF(E9<50,5,0). The formula =IF(E9>=50,0,5) would work just as well and give the same results. Can you see why =IF(E9>50,0,5) is wrong? What would happen if cell E9 contained a value of exactly £50?
- Finally, the formula in E11 should be =E9+E10. You could use =SUM(E9:E10) instead.

5 With these corrections, the spreadsheet should work properly for any sensible input data. Save any additional changes and close the spreadsheet.

Information: Nested IF functions

The City & Guilds outcomes say that you should be able to use simple IF statements. A formula with a simple IF function gives two possible results: one result if the condition is true and another result if the condition is false. It is possible that your assignment may suggest using a formula that gives three possible results. To do this you would need to use two IF functions nested one inside the other. There should be an option in the assignment to use two separate formulas each with a simple IF function instead of the single formula. The topic of nested IF functions is introduced here in case you meet it in an assignment and wish to take the option of using a formula that gives three possible results.

Suppose you want a spreadsheet user to enter a number between 10 and 20 inclusive in cell B3 of a spreadsheet. You want to make a message appear in cell C3 to say if the number they enter is too small, all right or too big.

You could start with the formula **=IF(B3<10,"Too small","All right")**. This goes part way towards a solution. Numbers less than 10 get a message "Too small". Numbers of 10 or more get a message "All right". These numbers need to be split up into numbers up to 20 and numbers greater than 20. You can do this with a second IF function **IF(B3<=20,"All right","Too big")**. This second IF function should be used only if the number is 10 or more, that is, only if the condition B3<10 is false. Whatever you put after the second comma in the original IF function will be carried out if the condition B3<10 is false. Instead of just displaying "All right", you could put the second IF function in there.
=IF(B3<10,"Too small",IF(B3<=20,"All right","Too big"))
Both IF functions need their closing brackets, so there are two brackets at the end of the formula.

Suppose the user enters the number 5. The condition B3<10 is true, so the instruction after the first comma of the outer IF function is carried out. The display is "Too small". →

Suppose the user enters the number 15. The condition B3<10 is false so the instruction after the second comma of the outer IF function is carried out. This instruction is **IF(B3<=20,"All right","Too big")**. The condition B3<=20 is true, so the instruction after the first comma of this inner IF function is carried out. The display is "All right".

Suppose the user enters the number 25. The condition B3<10 is false so the instruction after the second comma of the outer IF function is carried out. This instruction is **IF(B3<=20,"All right","Too big")**. The condition B3<=20 is false, so the instruction after the second comma of this inner IF function is carried out. The display is "Too big".

Task 4.16 — Use nested IF functions

Method

1   Create a new Excel workbook and save it with the name **NestedIF.xls**.
2   Enter data as shown in Figure 4.12.

	A	B
1	**Examples of nested IF functions**	
2		
3	Enter a number between 10 and 20	15
4		
5		
6	Enter the amount you want to invest	£100
7	Your interest rate	

Figure 4.12 The NestedIF spreadsheet

3   In cell C3, enter a formula that will tell you if your number is too small, all right, or too big. Take the phrase 'between 10 and 20' to mean 'between 10 and 20 inclusive' so that the numbers 10 and 20 count as all right.
The formula is:
=IF(B3<10,"Too small",IF(B3<=20,"All right","Too big"))
Make sure that you have two closing brackets at the end.
4   Cell B3 contains 15, so cell C3 should display **All right**.
5   Test the formula by entering different numbers in cell B3. Use numbers less than 10, including marginal numbers just less than 10. Cell C3 should display **Too small**.
6   Use the marginal numbers 10 and 20. Use numbers between 10 and 20. In each case cell C3 should display **All right**.
7   Use numbers greater than 20, and use a marginal number just greater than 20. In each case cell C3 should display **Too big**.
8   In cell B7, enter a formula to find the interest rate. The formula is:
=IF(B6<100,2%,IF(B6<1000,3%,4%))
9   Format cell B7 to show percentages. Format cell B6 to show 2 decimal places.
10   Test the formula by entering different values in cell B6. Use numbers less than 100, including the marginal value of 99.99. The interest rate should be 2%.
11   Use the marginal values of 100 and 999.99. Use values in between these. The interest rate should be 3%.
12   Use the marginal value of 1000 and use larger numbers. The interest rate should be 4%.
13   Save and close the spreadsheet.

→ Practise your skills 4.1: Exports2 spreadsheet

In this practice you will modify your Exports spreadsheet to use named ranges of cells in the formulas. You will also add some formulas containing IF functions.

If you cannot remember the methods, look back at the tasks earlier in this section.

1 Load Excel if it is not already open.

2 Open your Exports spreadsheet and save a copy with the name **Exports2.xls**. Work with Exports2.xls from now on.

3 Delete the formulas in cells B11 to E14 and B16 to E16.

4 Select cells B6 to B9 and give them the name **Year1**. Give appropriate ranges of cells the names **Year2**, **Year3** and **Year4**.

5 In cell B11, enter a formula to find the total for the year. Use the Year1 range name instead of a range of cell references. Find the totals for the other years, again using range names. You need to put in each formula separately and not copy them.

6 Enter formulas to find the average, maximum, minimum and count for each year. In each case, use a name instead of cell references.

7 Save the spreadsheet.

8 Enter a formula with an IF function in cell B18. If cell B16 shows the number 4, then cell B18 should display **OK**. Otherwise it should display **check**.

9 Copy the formula to cells C18, D18 and E18. All four cells should display OK.

10 Add your name in a header and add the file name in a footer.

11 Save the spreadsheet.

12 Delete the value in cell E7.

13 Print the spreadsheet on one sheet of paper.

14 Show the formulas and print them on one sheet of paper, showing gridlines and row and column headings. Make sure that all formulas show in full.

15 Hide the count formulas in row 16. Print again with these formulas hidden.

16 Close the spreadsheet without saving again.

→ Practise your skills 4.2: Food Survey2 spreadsheet

You will modify your Food Survey spreadsheet and add some formulas containing IF functions.

If you cannot remember the methods, look back at the tasks earlier in this section.

1 Load Excel if it is not already open.

2 Open your Food Survey spreadsheet and save a copy with the name **Food Survey2.xls**. Work with Food Survey2.xls from now on.

3 If the sheet is protected, remove the protection.

4 Go to cell D3. Enter a formula containing an IF function. If cell B3 is empty, then cell D3 should show the message "Enter your own name" otherwise cell D3 should show nothing.

5 Go to cell D4. Enter a formula containing an IF function. If cell B4 is empty, then cell D4 should show the message "Enter your own ID" otherwise cell D4 should show nothing.

6 Go to cell A19. Enter a formula containing an IF function. If the total number of fruit and vegetable portions is 35 or more then cell A19 should display "Good diet" otherwise it should display "Consider eating more fruit and veg". **Hint**: You can put a calculation in the condition part of an IF function, e.g. **B14+E15>=35**.

→

7 Save the spreadsheet.

8 Test the formulas in the spreadsheet. In particular, test the IF functions by changing the input data so that you can see that the results for 'then' and 'otherwise' appear correctly. Make any corrections.

9 Save again if necessary.

10 Print the spreadsheet showing formulas, showing gridlines and showing row and column headings.

11 Close the spreadsheet.

→ **Practise your skills 4.3:** Another quiz spreadsheet

You will set up a spreadsheet to record the results of a simple quiz with no bonus round. The spreadsheet will use an IF function to show which team has won.

1 Create a new spreadsheet and enter data and formatting as shown in Figure 4.13. Save the spreadsheet as **Another quiz.xls**.

	A	B	C	D
1	**Another quiz**			
2				
3		**Red team**	**Blue team**	**Green team**
4	Round 1	18	20	17
5	Round 2	12	17	16
6	Round 3	15	20	12
7	Round 4	13	15	19
8	**Total**			
9				
10	**Highest**			
11				
12	**Who won?**			

Figure 4.13 Another quiz spreadsheet

2 Enter a formula in cell B8 to find the total score for the red team. Replicate the formula to cells C8 and D8.

3 In cell B10, enter a formula using the MAX function to find the highest total score.

4 In cell B12, enter a formula using an IF function. If the total score for the red team is equal to the highest score, then display "Winner", otherwise display nothing. Use an absolute reference when you refer to the cell containing the highest score.

5 Replicate the formula from cell B12 to cells C12 and D12.

6 Save the spreadsheet.

7 The blue team should have the highest score of 72, and cell C12 should display Winner. Cells B12 and D12 should display nothing.

8 Test the spreadsheet by working out the calculations yourself for different sets of input data and comparing with the results of the formulas. Choose input data so that each team in turn is the winner. What happens if two or more teams have the same total score? Make any necessary corrections to formulas.

9 Restore the original input data and save again.

10 Add a header with your name and a footer with the date and the file name.

11 Unlock the cells containing the input data. Add any additional formatting you think suitable, such as background colour in cells or coloured fonts. What about giving cell B12 red font, C12 blue font and D12 green font?

12 Protect the sheet.

13 Save the spreadsheet and print a copy.

14 Print a copy showing formulas.

15 Remove protection from the sheet.

16 Give cell B10 the name **Highest**.

17 Edit the formula in cell B12 so that you use the name Highest instead of the absolute reference to cell B10. Replicate the formula to cells C12 and D12.

18 Check that the results are the same as before, protect the sheet, then save again.

19 Print the formulas again.

20 Close the spreadsheet.

→ Check your knowledge

1 What function could you use to display today's date in a cell?

2 Cell B3 contains the value 132.6718

Cell B4 contains the formula **=ROUND(B3,2)**
What is displayed in cell B4?

3 Cell B3 can be formatted to give the same display as cell B4. What is the difference between formatting and using the ROUND function to show a given number of decimal places?

4 Cell D4 contains the formula **=$B$1*D3**. You copy the formula to cell E4. What formula is now in cell E4?

5 In a different spreadsheet, cell B2 contains the VAT rate. The cell has been given the name **VATrate**. Cell D4 contains the formula **=D3*VATrate**. You copy the formula down to cell E4. What formula will be in cell E4?

6 Which two cells have their contents multiplied by the formula in cell E4?

7 Why might you use a named cell or a named range of cells in a spreadsheet?

8 Cell G6 contains the formula **=IF(F6>500,"Too big","All right")**. Cell F6 contains 500. What will be displayed in cell G6?

9 Cell G6 contains the formula **=IF(F6>500,"Too big","All right")**. Cell F6 contains 501. What will be displayed in cell G6?

10 A customer must pay a carriage charge of 10% of the order value on orders costing less than £80. The order value is in cell E15. The carriage charge is calculated using the following formula:

=IF(E15<80,E15*10%,0)

What values would you use in cell E15 to test the formula?

Consolidation 1

Scenario

The Environmental Science Information Service (ESIS) provides information on conservation, energy saving and waste management to organisations who pay an annual fee. The information comes mainly from articles in a large number of scientific and technical journals. ESIS keeps the names of the articles in a database. Anyone searching for information on a particular topic can enter a keyword and see a list of relevant articles. ESIS pays people called abstracters to read the articles and pick out keywords for the ESIS database. The abstracters may also write abstracts (short summaries) of the articles. These abstracts are published in a monthly magazine.

The abstracters are freelance workers who work at home. They receive a batch of articles each week. They are paid per article. There are different rates of pay for just picking keywords and for writing an abstract as well as picking keywords. Higher rates of pay apply if the articles are not in English. Each month an abstracter fills in an invoice showing the work done that month and the amount of payment due.

Your task is to produce a spreadsheet with an invoice form that an abstracter can use to enter the work done each week. The spreadsheet should calculate the pay due for each week's work, then calculate the monthly total.

1   Create a new Excel spreadsheet and save it as **Carruthers.xls.**

2   Enter data as shown.

	A	B	C	D	E	F	G
1	Environmental Science Information Service						
2	Keywords and abstracting by freelance workers						
3							
4	Rates of pay per article:						
5	£ 0.40	Type A	select keywords				
6	£ 0.80	Type B	write abstract and select keywords				
7	£ 0.90	Type C	foreign language - select keywords				
8	£ 1.20	Type D	foreign language - write abstract and select keywords				
9							
10	Name:	Mrs K Carruthers			Phone:	01908 528764	
11	Address:	25 Rainbow Way					
12		Milton Keynes					
13	Postcode:	MK14 3HM					
14							
15			Number of articles of each type in batch				
16	Batch ref.	Date	Type A	Type B	Type C	Type D	Pay for batch
17	99A001	04/01/2002	25	4	0	0	
18	99A002	11/01/2002	20	10	1	0	
19	99A003	18/01/2002	18	15	0	2	
20	99A004	25/01/2002	22	8	0	0	
21							
22							
23		Totals					

Figure 4.14 Carruthers spreadsheet

Hint:

You need to find the pay for each type of article and add them up. You will be using adding and multiplying in the same formula, so make sure you understand which will be carried out first. Take care with relative and absolute references. You could consider naming the cells containing the rates of pay and using the names in your formula.

3 Use suitable formatting to make the spreadsheet clear and easy to use. Cells A17 to F22 are data input cells and these should be formatted to look different from the other cells.

4 In cell G17, enter a formula that will work out the payment due for the batch. Replicate (copy) this formula to cells G18 to G22.

5 In cell C23, put in a formula to find the total number of articles of type A. Replicate this formula to cells D23 to G23.

6 In cell C25, enter the text "batches processed this month". In cell B25, enter a formula with a function that will count the number of batches.

7 If the total pay is less than £50 then a message should appear in cell A26, saying "Extra articles needed next month".

8 Add your name, the date, the file name and the sheet name in a footer.

9 Unlock data entry cells and protect the worksheet.

10 Test your spreadsheet using suitable test data. Work out the results yourself so that you can compare your own results with the results from the spreadsheet. When you have finished testing, restore the original data.

11 Save and print your spreadsheet.

12 Print again on one sheet of paper showing all formulas in full. Remove protection if necessary.

13 Display your results again and make sure that column widths are correctly set. (You may have needed to change column widths when showing formulas in full. You should be able to undo to restore the widths to their previous values.)

14 Save another copy of your spreadsheet with the name **Jackson.xls.**

15 Change the name, address and phone number on the sheet. The new entries are: Mr P Jackson, 18 Falmouth Drive, Milton Keynes, MK6 9FS. Phone 01908 511806. The sheet needs to be unprotected while you do this.

16 Batch references and numbers of articles for Mr Jackson are as follows. Make the changes.

Batch ref.	Date	Type A	Type B	Type C	Type D
02B001	04/01/02	18	1	0	0
02B002	11/01/02	21	2	0	0
02B003	18/01/02	20	12	0	0
02B004	25/01/02	20	5	0	0

Table 4.1 Batches for Mr Jackson

17 Save and print your Jackson spreadsheet.

18 Close the spreadsheet and close down Excel.

You will learn to

- Choose the right chart to suit different types of data
- Create a column chart from one or more series of data
- Print a chart on its own sheet
- Move and resize a chart on a worksheet
- Print a chart on a worksheet
- Identify the areas of a chart
- Format axes and gridlines
- Add data labels
- Format text
- Use colour and shading
- Use numbers as chart labels
- Create a bar chart
- Create a pie chart
- Select non-adjacent data for charting
- Create a line graph
- Create an XY (scatter) graph

Information: Why use graphs and charts?

The right picture is worth a thousand words – and the right chart can get a message across better than a sheet full of numbers. Most people find it easier to understand numerical information when it is presented as a chart. Use charts to display your spreadsheet data to the best advantage.

Information: Choosing the right chart

Excel provides many varieties of charts for different purposes. Choose your chart type with care. The right type of chart can display your information clearly at a glance. The wrong type of chart can give misleading information or just nonsense. The charts you will create are:

- column
- bar
- pie
- line
- XY or scatter.

Column chart

The column chart or vertical bar chart is a general purpose chart, commonly used in business. The heights of the columns show actual amounts. Heights can easily be compared. Figure 5.1 shows one series of data in one set of columns. It is easy to see the amount of exports to each country and to compare those amounts.

→

Exports in Year 1

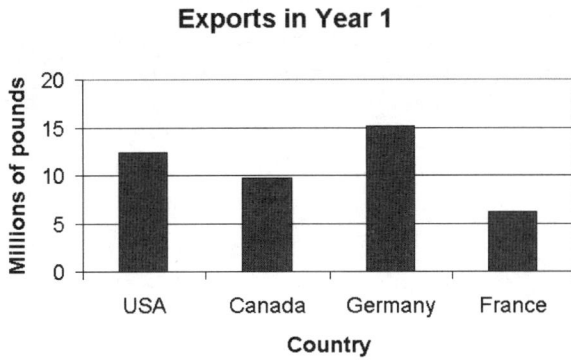

Figure 5.1 A column chart

Exports in 1998 and 1999

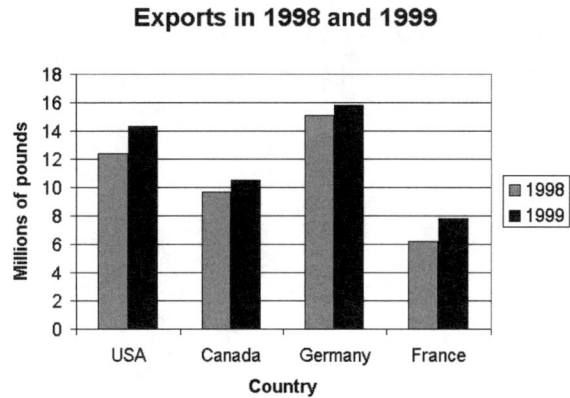

Figure 5.2 A column chart with two series of data

A column chart can show more than one series of data. Figure 5.2 shows exports in two different years. One data series holds the data for 1998, another data series holds the data for 1999.

Bar chart

A bar chart or horizontal bar chart is like a column chart on its side. Bar charts can be better for comparing the size of values. Column charts are better for showing variation over time.

Exports in 1998 and 1999

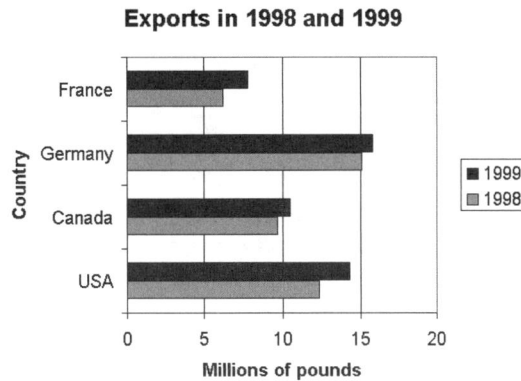

Figure 5.3 A bar chart

Pie chart

The pie chart does not normally show individual values of data items, though these can sometimes be added as labels. Instead it shows proportions or percentages. The whole chart represents the whole amount and the slices represent the percentages. In the following pie chart, we can see that 32% of the exports in the year 2001 went to Germany.

Exports 2001

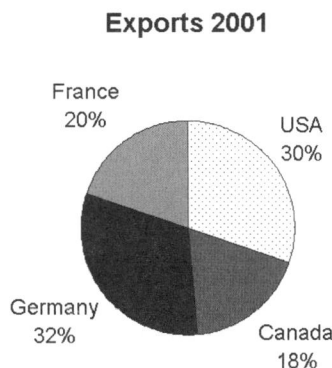

Figure 5.4 A pie chart

Line graph

The line graph is often used where a value changes with time. You can see how the values go up and down with time, and how quickly the values are changing. The first line graph shows one series of data: the price of shares in one company.

Share price of AJ Ltd

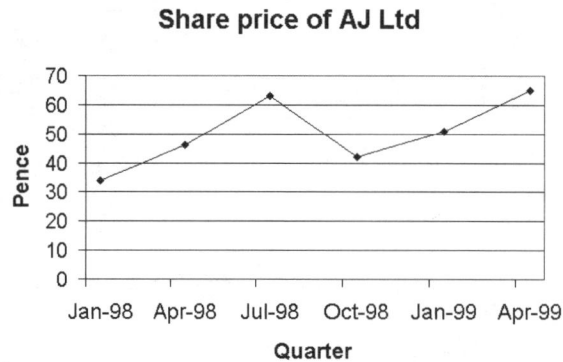

Figure 5.5 A line graph

A line graph can show more than one series of data. The second line graph shows share prices for three companies. Each company has its own line.

Share prices

Figure 5.6 A line graph with three series of data

XY graph

An XY graph, or scatter graph, is used where one value depends on another or where there are values at uneven intervals. A researcher bought 20 cups of coffee from different outlets and recorded the volume of coffee and the price to see if the price depended on the volume.

Coffee prices

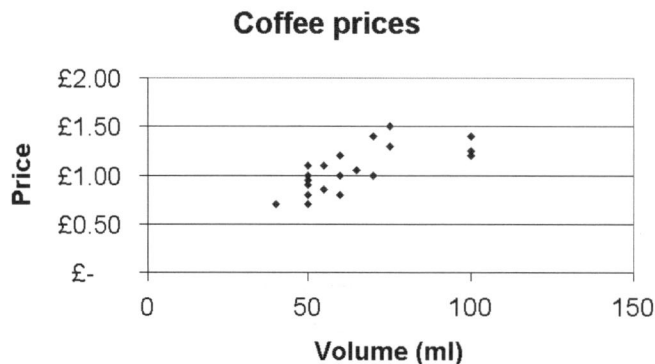

Figure 5.7 An XY scatter graph

Whichever type of chart you choose, keep it simple and keep it clear. There are many chart types available in Excel and some of them look very pretty, but they may not be the most suitable for your data. Some charts look colourful on screen, but are not clear when they are printed out in black and white.

Task 5.1 · Create a column chart from one series of data

You will create a column chart to show the exports to each country in the year 1998.

Method

1 Open your Exports.xls spreadsheet. It should look like Figure 5.8.

	A	B	C	D	E
1	**Exports**				29/06/2003
2					
3	Millions of pounds				
4					
5		**Year 1**	**Year 2**	**Year 3**	**Year 4**
6	**USA**	12.4	14.3	13.7	16.2
7	**Canada**	9.7	10.5	9.4	9.8
8	**Germany**	15.1	15.8	16.1	16.9
9	**France**	6.2	7.8	12.3	10.5
10					
11	**Total for year**	43.4	48.4	51.5	53.4
12	**Average for year**	10.9	12.1	12.9	13.4
13	**Maximum**	15.1	15.8	16.1	16.9
14	**Minimum**	6.2	7.8	9.4	9.8
15					
16	**Count entries**	4	4	4	4

Figure 5.8 The Exports spreadsheet

2 Select cells A6 to B9. You are selecting the names of the countries to use as labels on your chart, and the numbers that you want to plot: the export values for Year 1 only. Do not select any extra cells.

3 Click the Chart Wizard button on the toolbar

4 Step 1 of the Chart Wizard allows you to choose the type of chart you want from the list on the left. Column is the default. Select some of the other choices to see what chart types are offered, then return to the column chart.

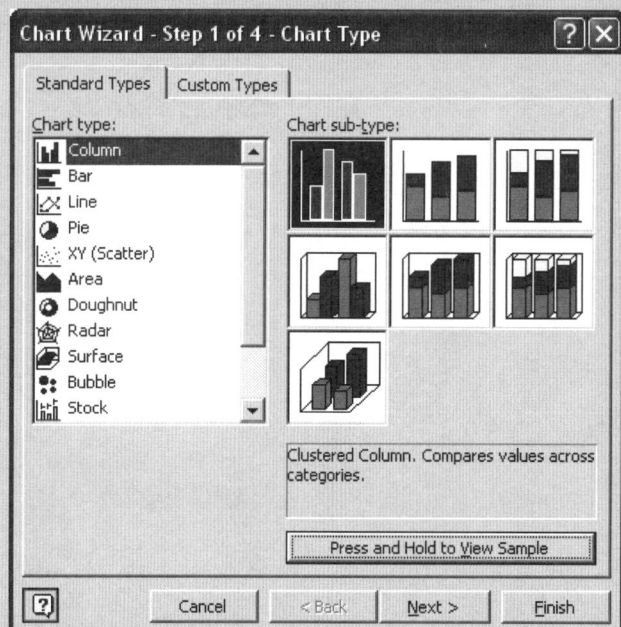

Figure 5.9 Step 1 of the Chart Wizard

5 On the right are the subtypes. You have a choice of three 2-D charts and four 3-D charts. Keep the default Clustered Column chart in the top left corner of the subtypes section.

6 There is a button labelled Press and Hold to View Sample. Point the mouse to this and hold down the left button to see a preview of your chart.

7 Click the button labelled Next.

8 Step 2 of the Chart Wizard lets you check that you have selected the right data for charting. The data range box shows the cells that you selected. You could change the selection at this stage if you wanted, but there is no need because the selection is correct.

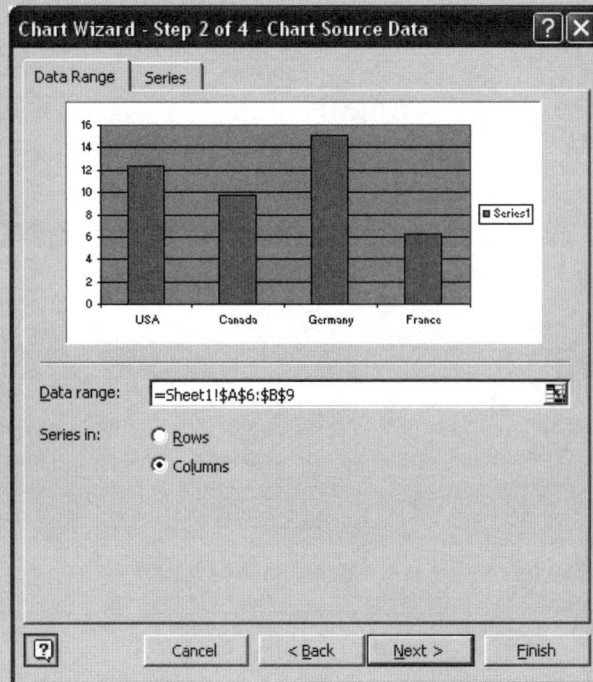

Figure 5.10 Step 2 of the Chart Wizard

9 Click on the Series tab near the top of the window. This shows your selection in more detail. You have one series of data selected for charting. This is known as Series1, and it has values =Sheet1!$B$6:$B$9, that is, cells B6 to B9. These are the numbers that are plotted as columns. The Category (X) labels are given as =Sheet1!$A$6:$A$9. Cells A6 to A9 contain the names of countries that are used as labels at the bottom of the columns. This window can be used to change the series and labels if necessary. Click Next.

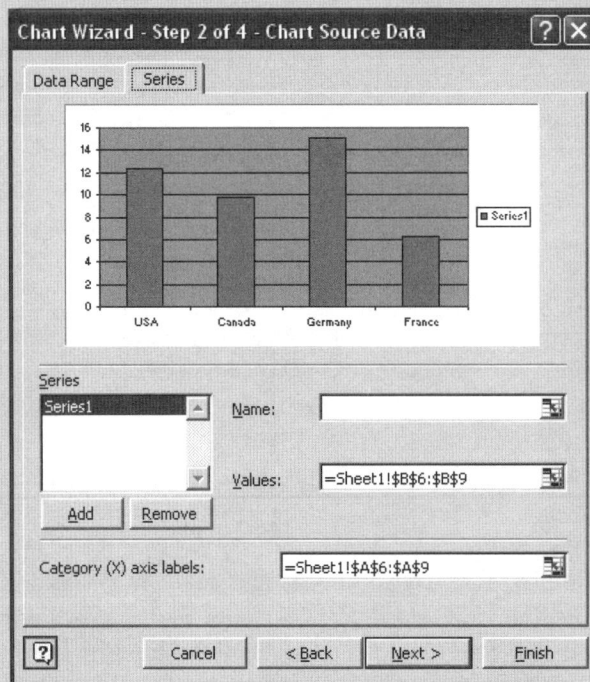

Figure 5.11 Step 2 of the Chart Wizard, Series tab

10 Step 3 lets you add titles and labels to your chart. The Titles tab should be in front.

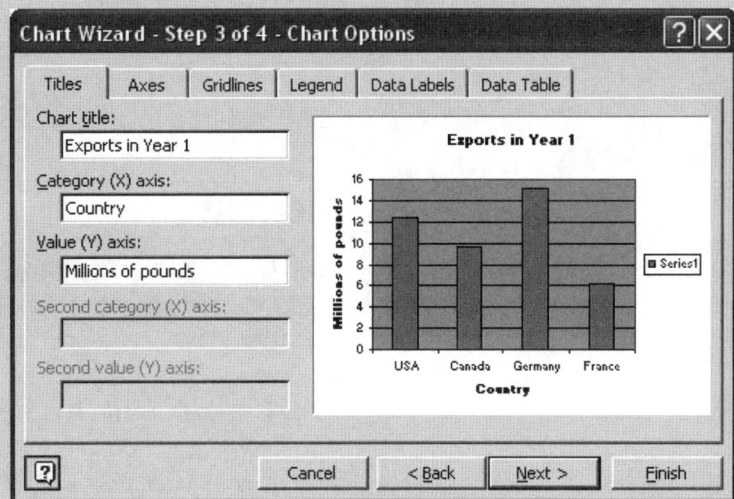

Figure 5.12 Step 3 of the Chart Wizard

11 Add the chart title 'Exports in Year 1'. Add a category (X) axis title 'Country'. Add a value (Y) axis title 'Millions of pounds'. These titles appear on the sample chart.

12 Click on the Axes tab at the top of the window and see how this dialogue lets you hide or show the labels on the X and Y axes by ticking or unticking the check boxes. Keep the default settings with both axes shown and the X axis set to automatic.

13 Click on the Gridlines tab. This dialogue lets you choose which gridlines to show. Try out the options, then return to the default with no X axis gridlines and only major gridlines on the Y axis.

14 Click on the Legend tab. Try placing the legend at the bottom, corner, top, right and left of the chart. Finally remove the tick from the Show Legend box. The current chart does not need a legend.

15 Click on the Data Labels tab. Try the effect of putting in series names, category names and values, then return to the default setting of no data labels.

16 Click the Data Table tab. Try the effect of showing the data table, then remove it again.

17 Click the Next button.

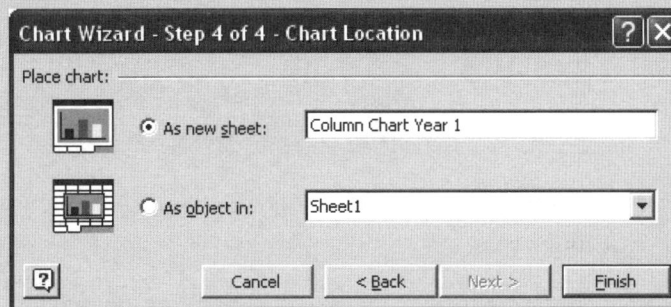

Figure 5.13 Step 4 of the Chart Wizard

18 Step 4 of the Chart Wizard lets you choose where you want to put the chart. It can have a new sheet of its own, or it can be placed on an existing worksheet. Select 'As new sheet' and enter a name for the new sheet: **Column Chart Year 1**.

19 Click the Finish button. The chart is created on its own sheet in the workbook.

20 Look at the sheet navigation tabs near the bottom of the screen and check that you can click on the tabs to move from the chart to Sheet1 and back.

Hint:

The X axis goes horizontally across the chart, usually at the bottom. The Y axis is vertical, usually at the left of the chart, though you can have a second Y axis on the right. If you forget which is X and which is Y, say 'X is a cross' (X is across).

Task 5.2   Print a chart on its own sheet

You will put in a header and footer and print your column chart.

Method

1. A chart on its own sheet needs its own header and footer. It does not share a header and footer with the original worksheet. Click on the View menu and select Header and Footer from the drop down list.
2. The Page Setup window appears with its Header and Footer tab in front. Click on the button labelled Custom Header.
3. Key in your name in the left-hand section of the header window and click OK.
4. Click on the button labelled Custom Footer.
5. Enter the date in the left section of the footer. Enter the file name, a space and the sheet name in the centre section. Click OK. Click OK again to close the Page Setup window.
6. Preview your chart using the Print Preview button on the toolbar.
7. Check the display, then click the Print button.
8. Keep the default settings in the Print dialogue box and click OK to print the chart.
9. Save the workbook by clicking the Save button on the toolbar. This saves all the sheets, including the sheet with the chart, together in one file.

Task 5.3   Create a column chart from several series of data

You will create a column chart to show exports to the four countries in each of four years.

Method

1. Start with your Exports spreadsheet, on the sheet showing the data. Select cells A5 to E9. You are including the country names and the year numbers as labels as well as the numbers that you want to plot as columns.
2. Click the Chart Wizard button on the toolbar.
3. In step 1 of the chart, keep the default settings of Column chart and Clustered column subtype. Use the button labelled Press and Hold to View Sample. The sample should appear similar to Figure 5.14.

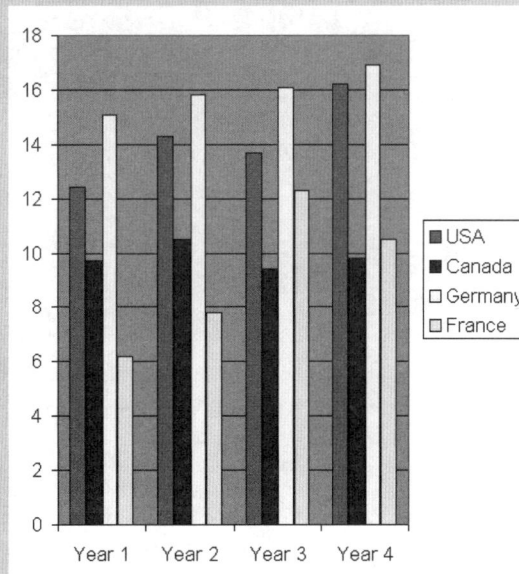

Figure 5.14 Sample of column chart

4 Click the Next button.

5 In step 2, the option Series in Rows is selected. In the original table there is a row for USA values. The values from this row form a series with columns all the same colour and a series name, USA, in the legend. Similarly, the Canada row forms a series, the Germany row forms a series and the France row forms a series. The years are shown as X axis labels.

6 Select the Series in Columns option. The display changes. In the original table there is a column for Year I values. These values now form a series with their columns all the same colour and the series name, Year I, in the legend. Similarly, the Year 2 values form a series, the Year 3 values form a series and the Year 4 values form a series. The country names are shown as X axis labels.

7 You can choose to have the series in rows or columns, depending on the effect you want to produce. This time, keep the series in columns and click the Next button.

8 Click the Titles tab to bring it to the front. Key in a title: **Exports**. Key in the Category (X) axis title: **Country**. Key in the Value (Y) axis title: **Millions of pounds**.

9 Look at the other tabs if you wish, but leave the settings unchanged. Click the Next button.

10 In step 4, keep the default value: Place chart as object in Sheet I. Click Finish.

11 The chart appears on top of the worksheet. It is selected, and has small black squares, the resize handles, in the corners and in the middles of the sides.

12 Save the workbook.

Task 5.4 — Move and resize a chart on a worksheet

You will move the chart and change its size. You will also see how the chart is linked to the data on the worksheet.

Hint:

Take care not to point to the central part of the chart or to any of the titles when you move the chart, otherwise you may move parts of the chart within its frame.

Hint:

Do not delete any data that has been used for charting. The chart columns will vanish too.

Method

1 Point the mouse to the outer white area of the chart. Hold down the left button and drag the chart to a clear area of the sheet so that it does not cover up the entries in the cells.
2 Make sure that the chart is selected, with its resize handles showing. Point the mouse to the resize handle in the bottom right corner of the chart. The mouse pointer should change to a double-headed arrow. Hold the left mouse button down as you drag the mouse down and to the right to make the chart larger.
3 Adjust the chart until you can see the data on the sheet at the same time as the chart.
4 Go to cell B6. Change the value for the USA, Year 1 to 1.5. Watch the chart as you press Enter to fix the new value. The bar for USA, Year 1 should change its height.
5 Change the value back to the original 12.4 and watch the column return to its original height. The chart is linked to its original data. Any changes in the data are reflected in the chart.

Task 5.5 — Print a chart on a worksheet

When a chart is on a worksheet, you can print the chart alone or you can print the chart with the worksheet.

Method

1 Click on the chart to select it.
2 Select Header and Footer from the View menu, and put in a header with your name and a footer with the date.
3 Click the Preview button on the toolbar.
4 Print the chart. It should print alone as if it were on its own sheet.
5 Click on one of the cells on the worksheet so that the chart is not selected.
6 Click the Preview button on the toolbar. The chart is displayed with the sheet.
7 You may wish to close the preview so that you can adjust the position or size of the chart on the sheet to give a good display. You may also wish to add a header and footer to the sheet if it does not have them already. Preview again.
8 When you are satisfied with the preview, print the sheet with its chart.
9 Save the workbook.

Each area of the chart has its own name and can be selected for formatting or editing. You can also return to each of the steps of the Wizard to make changes.

Method

1   Select the chart.
2   Point the mouse at each area of the chart in turn. Hold the mouse still without clicking and a yellow label should appear.

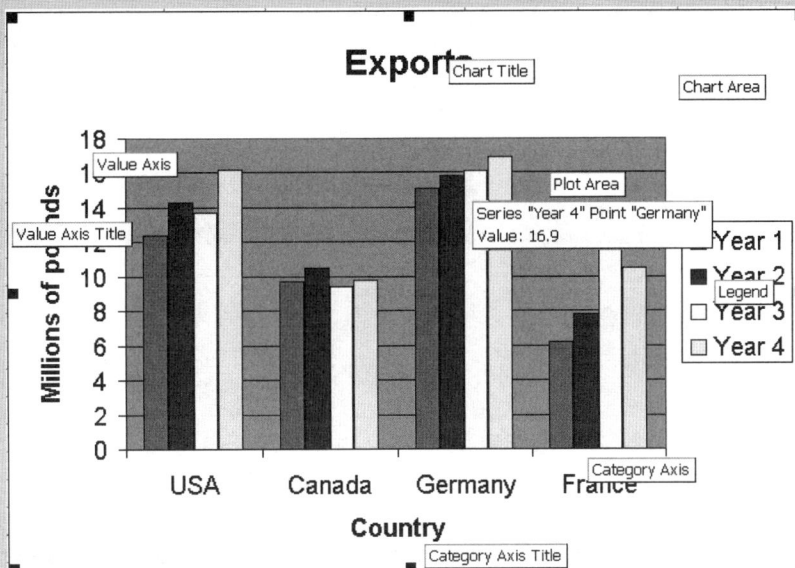

Figure 5.15 Areas of a chart

3   Identify the Chart Area, the Plot Area, the Chart Title, the Value Axis Title, the Value Axis, the Category Axis Title, the Category Axis, the Legend and the individual data points such as 'Series "Year 4" Point "Germany" Value: 16.9'. Labels appear one at a time. You cannot show them all at once. The labels in Figure 5.15 have been added in later.

4   Right click on some of these areas. In each case a pop-up menu appears. The options available on the menu are not always the same. They depend on the area of the chart that you clicked on. Close the pop-up menu by left clicking in the outer chart area. You will use some of these pop-up menus later.

5   Make sure that your chart is still selected. Click on the Chart menu on the menu bar at the top of the screen. Select Chart Type from the drop down list. You see a dialogue box that is the same as the first step of the Chart Wizard. You can use this dialogue box to change the chart type of your existing chart. Cancel the dialogue box.

6   Click on the Chart menu and select Source Data. The dialogue box that appears is the same as step 2 of the Chart Wizard. You can use this dialogue to change the data that you include in your chart or swap between series in rows or columns. Cancel the dialogue box.

7   Click on the Chart menu and select Chart Options. The dialogue box that appears is the same as step 3 of the Chart Wizard. You can change the titles. You can change the display of axes and gridlines. You can add or remove a legend, data labels or a data chart. Cancel the dialogue box.

8 Click on the Chart menu and select Location. The dialogue box that appears is the same as step 4 of the Chart Wizard. You can move your chart from the worksheet to a sheet of its own or move a chart on to a worksheet. Select 'As new sheet' and give the new sheet the name 'Column All Years' as shown in Figure 5.16. Click OK. Your chart is now on a sheet of its own.

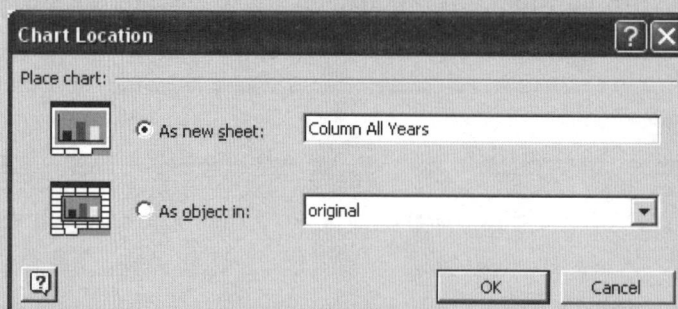

Figure 5.16 Moving the chart to its own sheet

Task 5.7 Format axes and gridlines

Method

1 Start with your column chart showing exports in all four years. This chart should now be on its own sheet.

2 Right click on the Value Axis and choose Format Axis from the pop-up menu. The Format Axis dialogue box appears.

3 Click on the Scale tab. At present Excel is choosing the maximum and minimum values on the scale automatically. Change the maximum value to 20. Change the Major unit to 5. Notice that the ticks are removed from the auto box opposite the maximum and major unit values.

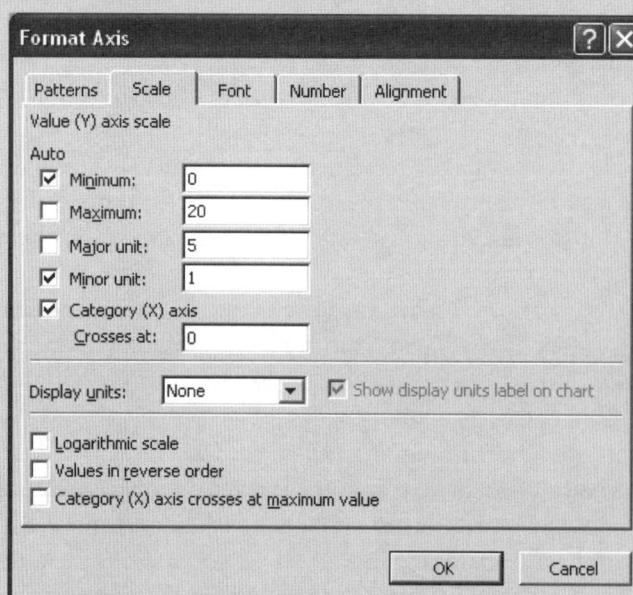

Figure 5.17 Changing the maximum and major unit on the Value axis

4 Click OK. Check that the scale now goes from 0 to 20 on the Value (Y) axis. It should now go up in 5s instead of 2s.

5   Click on the Chart menu and select Chart Options. Click on the Gridlines tab.

6   Click in the Value Axis minor gridlines box and click OK. You now have gridlines at intervals of 1 instead of 5 on the axis. The gridlines at 5, 10, 15 and 20 are major gridlines. The others are minor gridlines.

7   Right click on one of the minor gridlines. Select Format Gridlines from the pop-up menu. Click the Patterns tab to bring it to the front.

8   Click on the arrow by the style box to show the drop down list, and select a dotted line. You could choose a different colour if you wish. Click OK.

Task 5.8   Add data labels, change fonts and colours

Method

1   Click on the Chart menu and select Chart Options. Click on the Data Labels tab.

2   Select the Value option and click OK. Values appear at the top of the columns.

3   Right click on the chart title and select Format Chart Title from the pop-up list.

4   Click on the Font tab, and choose a font, style, size and colour. Click OK.

5   Right click on the outer chart area. Select Format Chart Area from the pop-up list.

6   Click on the Patterns tab. The section on the left of the window lets you choose a border for the chart area. The section on the right lets you choose a background colour.

7   Select a background colour from the palette of colours.

8   Click the Fill Effects button.

9   Explore the gradients, textures and patterns available to you. You can also use a background picture if you have a suitable image file available. Click OK to see the effect. Select Format Chart Area again to make further changes.

10 You can use colours and patterns in the inner Plot area in the same way as in the outer Chart area. Try it out.

11 You can select series of columns and change their colour or add a pattern. Try this out.

12 Select suitable colours and/or patterns to make a completed chart. Avoid using too many colours or too many complicated fills or patterns.

13 Save the workbook and print a copy of your completed chart.

Hint:

You can format the font of the axis labels in the same way as the chart title.

Hint:

If you are printing in black and white then choose colours that will print clearly in shades of grey. You may be able to use patterns to make the columns of different series show up clearly. Some printers may not print patterns well, especially if they have not been set up properly. Try a printout and see what happens.

You may run into problems if the labels for your chart are numbers. You need to know how to recognise and avoid these problems.

Method

1. Return to your original worksheet containing the data by clicking on its tab near the bottom of the screen.
2. Change the contents of cells B5 to E5 so that they show year numbers 1998, 1999, etc. rather than Year 1, Year 2, etc., as shown in Figure 5.18. Key in **Year** in cell A5.

	A	B	C	D	E
1	**Exports**				29/06/2003
2					
3	Millions of pounds				
4					
5	**Year**	**1998**	**1999**	**2000**	**2001**
6	**USA**	12.4	14.3	13.7	16.2
7	**Canada**	9.7	10.5	9.4	9.8
8	**Germany**	15.1	15.8	16.1	16.9
9	**France**	6.2	7.8	12.3	10.5

Figure 5.18 Part of worksheet with year numbers

3. Select cells A5 to E9. Click the Chart Wizard button on the toolbar.
4. Use the Press and Hold to View Sample button.
5. You should see four columns with a height of about 2000 in the Year section. The USA, Canada and other sections have columns so small that they do not show up on the scale. Excel has plotted the year numbers, 1998, 1999, etc., as columns. This is not what you want. It is possible to move on to step 2 of the Wizard and make corrections in the Series window, but there is a simpler way of stopping Excel from plotting the year numbers.
6. Click the Cancel button to stop the Wizard.
7. Go to cell B5 and key in **'1998**. Include the single quote. The single quote tells Excel to treat the entry as text and not as a number. The single quote will not be displayed in the cell.
8. Key in the other year numbers again, this time with a single quote in front.
9. Select cells A5 to E9. Click the Chart Wizard button on the toolbar.
10. Use the Press and Hold to View Sample button.
11. This time the columns should display correctly and the years should not be plotted. Instead the years are used as labels.
12. You need not continue with this chart unless you want the practice. Stop the Wizard by using the Cancel button.

Hint:

If cell A5 is empty, Excel will not plot the years even if they are entered as numbers. It will use the years as labels.

Hint:

Ignore the green triangle that appears in the cell when you key in '1998. Excel is warning you that a number is being treated as text.

Task 5.10 — Create a bar chart

You will create a different type of chart using the same basic data as before. Bar charts are similar to column charts but the bars are horizontal instead of vertical.

Method

1	Start with your Export.xls spreadsheet open and Sheet1, containing your data, in front. On your Export worksheet, select cells A5 to E9.
2	Click the Chart Wizard button.
3	In step 1 of the Chart Wizard, select Bar from the list of chart types. Keep the default subtype of clustered bar. View the sample. Click Next.
4	There are no changes to make in step 2. Click Next.
5	In step 3, click the Titles tab. Key in the title: **Exports**. Key in the Category Axis Title: **Year**. Key in the Value Axis Title: **Millions of pounds**.
6	There are no other changes. Click Next.
7	In step 4, choose to put the chart on its own new sheet called **Bar**. Click Finish.
8	Add a header and a footer showing your name, the date and the file name. Check that you can find the parts of the chart as you did for the column chart. You can change gridlines, font, colour and patterns just as you did with the column chart.
9	Save the workbook.
10	Print your bar chart.
11	Switch back to the worksheet containing your data.

Task 5.11 — Create a pie chart

You will create a pie chart to show the percentage of the total exports that went to each country in 1998. You will 'explode' one or more slices to emphasise them. A pie chart only shows one series of data.

Method

1	On your Exports worksheet, select cells A6 to B9 so that you have the numbers that you want to plot, and the country names to use as labels.
2	Click on the Chart Wizard button.
3	In step 1 of the Wizard, select Pie as the chart type, and keep the default subtype. Click Next.
4	There are no changes to be made in step 2. Click Next.
5	In step 3, key in a title: **Exports in 1998**. Pie charts do not have X and Y axes, so there are no axes titles.
6	Still in step 3, click on the Data Labels tab. Try out the options for labels: series name, category name, value and percentage. Keep the category name and percentage options. Click Next.

7   In step 4, choose to place the pie chart as an object on the worksheet. Click Finish.

8   Move and resize the chart on the sheet so that it is large enough to give a good display and does not hide any of the data on the sheet.

9   Click into the pie itself to select it. A resize handle appears on each 'slice'. Point the mouse at the Canada slice, hold down the left mouse button and drag outwards. The pie 'explodes' as all the slices move outwards.

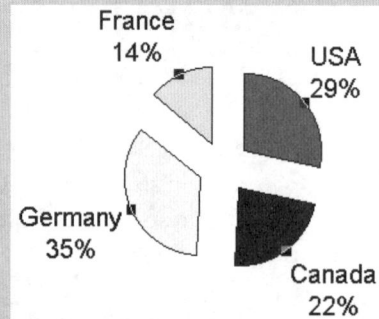

Figure 5.19 Exploded pie chart

10   Drag the Canada slice back towards the centre of the pie so that all the slices go back to their original positions.

11   The pie area should still be selected. Click again on the Canada slice. This time only the Canada slice should be selected, with several resize handles round it. Drag the Canada slice outwards. This slice moves but the other slices stay in place.

12   Save the workbook. Print the worksheet with the pie chart on it.

Task 5.12   Select non-adjacent data for charting

You will create a pie chart to show exports for the year 2001. This time the numbers you want to plot are not next to their labels.

Method

1   Start with your Exports worksheet as usual. You need to select the country names in cells A6 to A9, and you need to select the values for the year 2001 in cells E6 to E9, but without selecting any other cells.

2   Select cells A6 to A9. Hold down the Ctrl key on the keyboard as you select cells E6 to E9. You now have two non-adjacent ranges of cells selected.

3   Click the Chart Wizard button.

4   Use the Wizard to create a pie chart with the title **Exports in 2001**, showing labels and percentages. Put the chart on its own sheet.

5   Select the pie area, then click again on one slice to select it. Right click on the slice and select Format Data Point from the pop-up menu. Give the slice a colour or pattern that would give a clear display either in colour or in black and white. Do the same with the other slices, giving each a different colour or pattern.

6 Give the chart a header and footer showing your name, the date and the file name. Print the chart. Save the workbook.

7 Switch back to the sheet containing your data.

Task 5.13 | Create a line graph

You will create a line graph showing how the exports to the four countries have changed over the four years 1998 to 2001.

Method

1 On your Exports worksheet, select cells A5 to E9.
2 Click the Chart Wizard button.
3 In step 1, choose the Line chart type and keep the default subtype that shows lines and data points.
4 There should be no changes in step 2. Check that year numbers are shown on the X axis and that there is a line for each country.
5 In step 3, give the chart a title: **Exports 1998 to 2001**. Give the X axis the title **Year**. Give the Y axis the title **Millions of pounds**.
6 In step 4, place the chart in its own new sheet called **Exports Line**.
7 You can select and change the parts of a line graph just as you can for a column chart. Give the main title a different font and size.
8 Make the numbers on the Y axis go from 0 to 20.
9 Put a coloured background in the chart area.
10 Select each line in turn. Change its colour and the colour of the symbol on the line.
11 Add a header and footer, then print the chart.
12 Save the workbook and close it.

Hint:

To format any part of a chart, select the part. Right click on it and choose Format . . . from the pop-up menu.

Remember:

Do take breaks. This would be another convenient time before you start Task 5.14.

Task 5.14 | Create an XY (scatter) graph

You will create a graph to show the growth of a sunflower plant. The height of the plant was measured at irregular intervals so an XY graph is better than a line graph. The data points follow each other in order, so it makes sense to put a line through them.

Method

1 Create a new spreadsheet as shown in Figure 5.20. Save the spreadsheet as **Sunflower.xls.**
2 Select cells A4 to B13.
3 Click the Chart Wizard button.
4 In step 1 of the Wizard, select XY (scatter) from the list of chart types. Select the second subtype that shows the data points connected by a smoothed line.
5 There should be no changes needed in step 2.

	A	B
1	**Sunflower**	
2		
3	**Date**	**Height (cm)**
4	30/03/2002	0
5	12/05/2002	12
6	20/06/2002	44
7	01/07/2002	52
8	15/07/2002	90
9	25/07/2002	104
10	01/08/2002	125
11	04/08/2002	160
12	10/08/2002	195
13	20/08/2002	203

Figure 5.20 Sunflower spreadsheet

6   In step 3, give your chart the title **Sunflower**. Give the X axis the title **Date**. Give the Y axis the title **Height (cm)**. Remove the legend.

7   In step 4, place the chart as an object on the worksheet.

8   Move and resize the chart so that it is large enough to display well without hiding the data on the sheet.

9   Add a suitable header and footer.

10   Save the workbook.

11   Print preview and move or resize the chart if necessary, then print the sheet.

12   Close the workbook.

Information: Choosing and enhancing a graph or chart

You have learned how to create a variety of charts and how to enhance them by the use of fonts, colours and patterns. Remember that the purpose of a chart is to get over a message about your data. Enhancements should help the message and not just look pretty. Excel provides many other types and subtypes of charts, including 3-D types. When choosing a type of chart, think about how well the chart suits your data, and how clearly it conveys your message, not just how the chart looks.

Information: Selecting spreadsheet data for a graph or chart

The key to trouble-free charting is to select the right data on the spreadsheet before you start. Your series of data for charting need to be organised into a block of rows and columns on the spreadsheet. Select only the block of cells you want and no more. There should be no empty rows or columns within the block. Excel will try to plot any empty rows or columns as zero values on your chart. This will leave gaps in a column or bar chart. If you try to create a pie chart you may find that there is nothing visible at all.

If you select the wrong cells, it is possible to make corrections in step 2 of the Wizard, and select the right cells for each series and for the labels. This can be awkward. It is much better to start off with the right cells selected in the first place.

→

You might like to try this out for interest. Open your Exports spreadsheet. Insert an empty column between the country names and the 1998 values. Insert more empty columns between the values for the different years. Insert empty rows between the country names. Select all the data. Try making a column chart. Try making a pie chart. Can you correct your charts using step 2 of the Wizard? Close the spreadsheet without saving. This should convince you that empty rows or columns are a bad idea when charting.

When you select non-adjacent columns of data for charting, make sure that each column contains the same number of cells and that the tops of the columns are level with each other. You could select cells A3 to A6 and D3 to D6, but you should not select cells A4 to A6 and D3 to D6 because they do not have the same number of cells. You should not select A3 to A6 and D4 to D7 because the tops of the columns are not level. The same ideas apply when you select non-adjacent rows. They must contain the same number of cells and start level with each other.

→ Practise your skills 5.1: Unit trust spreadsheet

You will create some charts to show how the value of certain investments has changed over the last few years.

1 Load Excel if it is not already open.

2 Create a new spreadsheet as shown in Figure 5.21. Save the workbook as **Unit Trust.xls.**

	A	B	C	D
1	Unit Trust Investments			
2				
3	Date	Growth fund	Income fund	General fund
4	30/06/1997	£ 1,000.00	£ 1,000.00	£ 1,000.00
5	31/12/1997	£ 1,033.71	£ 1,085.53	£ 1,031.58
6	30/06/1998	£ 1,247.18	£ 1,184.99	£ 1,052.63
7	31/12/1998	£ 1,141.27	£ 1,103.10	£ 1,035.69
8	30/06/1999	£ 1,187.67	£ 1,179.83	£ 1,096.57
9	31/12/1999	£ 1,286.60	£ 1,337.71	£ 1,153.81
10	30/06/2000	£ 1,287.75	£ 1,217.71	£ 1,160.13
11	31/12/2000	£ 1,247.37	£ 1,218.11	£ 1,172.81
12	30/06/2001	£ 1,047.09	£ 1,075.35	£ 1,019.97
13	31/12/2001	£ 982.57	£ 1,024.21	£ 983.41
14	30/06/2002	£ 808.76	£ 845.88	£ 749.74

Figure 5.21 Unit Trust spreadsheet

3 Create a line graph to show how the value of the investment in the Growth fund has changed from 30/6/97 to 30/06/02. Add suitable headings and labels. The graph should be on its own sheet. Call the sheet **Growth fund line**.

4 Add a header and footer to show your name, the date, the file name and the sheet name.

5 Print the graph.

6 Create a line graph to show how the value of the investment in all three funds has changed from 30/6/97 to 30/06/02. Add suitable headings and labels. There should be a legend showing the names of the funds. The graph should be on its own sheet. Call the sheet **All funds line**.

7 Add a suitable header and footer.

8 Format the Y axis so that the scale has a minimum value of 600 and a maximum value of 1400.

9 Format the X axis so that the major unit is 6 months.

10 Format backgrounds, lines and the markers on the lines to give a clear display in a black and white printout.

11 Save the workbook and print the graph.

12 Close the workbook.

13 On a sheet of paper, write down why a line graph is a suitable choice for displaying the data in this workbook.

→ **Practise your skills 5.2:** Cereals spreadsheet

You will create some charts to illustrate the sales of cereals.

1 Load Excel if it is not already open.

2 Create a new spreadsheet as shown in Figure 5.22. Save the workbook as **Cereals.xls.** Save again regularly as you work.

	A	B	C	D	E	F
1	**Sales of Cereals**					
2	In metric tonnes					
3						
4	Year	1998	1999	2000	2001	Total
5	Corn flakes	35	38	40	41	
6	Wheat biscuits	27	24	21	22	
7	Sugared rice	18	25	24	21	
8	Fruit muesli	29	26	20	24	

Figure 5.22 Cereals spreadsheet

3 Put in formulas to find the total weight of each type of cereal sold.

4 Create a column chart to show the sales of all four types of cereal for all four years. Do not include the totals. Make sure that you do not chart the year numbers. They should be used as labels on the X axis. The cereal names should be in a legend. Put in suitable headings and labels on the axes. Put the chart on the same sheet as the data.

5 Adjust the size and position of the chart so that the chart and the data can be displayed on one sheet of paper in portrait orientation.

6 Format the chart to give a clear display when printed in black and white. Add a suitable header and footer. Print the sheet showing the data and the chart.

7 Create a line graph to show how the sale of each type of cereal has changed over the years. There should be four lines, one for each cereal. Year numbers should be shown on the X axis and the cereal names should be shown in a legend. Include suitable titles. Put the chart on a sheet of its own and call the sheet **Line graph**.

8 Format the chart so that the lines are clearly distinguishable in black and white. Add a suitable header and footer and print the line graph.

9 Create a pie chart to show the sales of each type of cereal in 1998 as a percentage of the total sales in 1998. (You do not need to calculate the total sales figure for 1998. Just chart the numbers and use the cereal names as labels.) Include a suitable title. Show labels and percentages as data labels but do not show the legend. Put the pie chart on the same sheet as the data.

10 Adjust the size and position of the chart so that the pie chart is below the existing chart on the sheet and is a similar size.

11 Explode the largest section of the pie chart.

12 Format the font to make it a suitable size. Format the colours of the pie chart and use patterns to make the sections clearly distinguishable both in colour on the screen and in a black and white printout.

→

13 Print the chart by itself, without the rest of the sheet, showing a suitable header and footer.

14 Create a second pie chart using the total sales figures instead of the figures for 1998. Format it in the same way as the 1998 chart. Print the chart.

15 Close the workbook.

→ Check your knowledge

1 A spreadsheet has a list of daily temperature readings from a weather station. It shows the dates and the temperatures at midday. The temperatures are to be displayed as a chart or graph. Which type of chart or graph would you choose, and why?

2 In a survey, 1000 people were asked if they agree that Great Britain should join the European single currency. A spreadsheet shows the number of people who agree strongly, agree a bit, disagree a bit, or disagree strongly. Which type of chart or graph would you choose to display the data, and why?

3 In a survey, smokers were asked their annual income and the number of cigarettes they smoke in a week. The researcher wanted to find out if people who have more money smoke more cigarettes. Which type of chart or graph would you choose to display the data, and why?

4 500 people were asked how they travel to work: car, bus, train, bike, walk or other. A spreadsheet shows the methods of transport and the number of people using each method. Which type of chart or graph would you choose to display the data, and why?

5 You select a block of spreadsheet cells and create a chart. There are empty rows in your selection. Why does this give a problem?

6 You want to plot a column chart to show the number of college students enrolled in 1999, 2000 and 2001. You find that instead of showing as labels on the X axis, the year numbers have been plotted as columns. What should you do?

7 What is an exploded pie chart?

8 You are using the Chart Wizard and click Finish by mistake. Can you get the Wizard back to carry on using it?

9 You have a chart on a worksheet. You want to print the chart and the worksheet together, but when you preview you can only see the chart. Why is this?

10 You have a chart on a worksheet but you want to move it to a sheet of its own. Can you do this?

Section 6

Using copy and link to import and extract data

You will learn to

- Work with worksheets within a workbook
- Copy values and formulas from one worksheet to another
- Make links between worksheets using formulas
- Copy from one workbook file to another
- Make links between workbooks using formulas
- Copy a chart from one workbook to another keeping a link
- Copy a picture of a chart from one workbook to another
- Use hyperlinks
- Save edited and linked workbooks with suitable names
- Identify the differences between copying data values, linking data values and pasting data objects

In this section you will copy data in various ways. You already know how to copy and move data and formulas from one part of a worksheet to another using relative and absolute references. In this section you will copy data from one sheet to another within a workbook, and from one workbook to another. Copied data can keep a link with the original data so that it changes when the original changes, or the copy can be independent so that there is no link. Before copying data between worksheets you need to be able to use more than one worksheet in a workbook.

Information: Worksheets and workbooks

An Excel file saves a complete Excel workbook, which can contain several worksheets. You can swap from one worksheet to another by clicking on the sheet navigation tabs at the bottom of the window. You will know from your work with charts that charts can have their own sheets in a workbook.

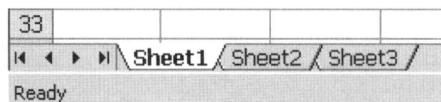

Figure 6.1 Sheet navigation tabs

Another way of moving from one sheet to another in a workbook is to hold down the Ctrl key and use the Page Down or Page Up keys. Page Down moves to the next sheet. Page Up moves to the previous sheet.

When you create a new workbook it starts with a default number of sheets. This default is probably three. The default number can be changed so that Excel can start each new workbook with your chosen number of sheets.

Sheets can be inserted and deleted, renamed, copied and moved. You can select several sheets at a time and enter data, add headers and footers or print them all at once.

Method

1. Open your Avondale.xls workbook and save it as **Avondale2.xls.** Use Avondale2.xls from now on.
2. Your workbook should have a worksheet, called Sheet1, that displays an invoice for a customer. There should also be blank worksheets called Sheet2 and Sheet3. Select Sheet1.
3. Click on the Insert menu and select Worksheet from the drop down list. A new worksheet called Sheet4 should appear with its tab to the left of Sheet1.
4. Here is an alternative way of inserting a sheet. Select Sheet1 again. Right click on the tab of Sheet1. Select Insert from the pop-up menu that appears. This time you should see a dialogue box offering you a choice of possible sheets and whole workbooks to insert. Keep the default option, which should be called Worksheet, and click OK. The new worksheet should appear just to the left of Sheet1.
5. With your new sheet selected, click on the Edit menu and select Delete Sheet from the drop down list. If the sheet contains any data there is a warning message and you need to click Delete to confirm the deletion. If the sheet is empty it just disappears.
6. Right click the tab of Sheet4. Select Delete from the pop-up menu. Again you see the warning. Click OK and Sheet4 will disappear.
7. Click on the tab of Sheet2 to select it, and then hold down the Ctrl key as you click on the tab of Sheet3. Both tabs should be white to show that they are both selected.
8. Delete both Sheet2 and Sheet3 together using either the menu method or the right click method.
9. Sheet1 should now be the only sheet left, and it should show the invoice for J K Jarvis.

Task 6.2 | Copy and rename worksheets

Method

1. Right click the tab of Sheet1. Select Move or Copy from the pop-up menu. The Move or Copy dialogue box should appear.

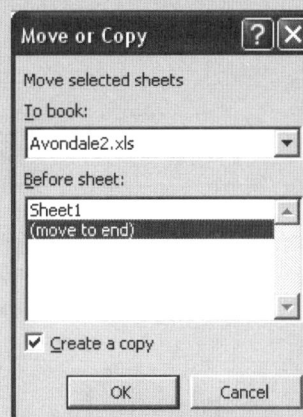

Figure 6.2 The Move or Copy dialogue box

2. Click to place a tick in the check box labelled 'Create a copy'. Select (move to end) in the list labelled 'Before sheet:'. Notice that you are copying within the Avondale2.xls workbook but there is an option that lets you choose to copy to a different workbook. Click OK.

3 A new sheet called Sheet1 (2) should appear. It should look exactly like Sheet1.

4 Right click on the tab of Sheet1. Select Rename from the pop-up list.

5 The sheet name is selected. Key in **Jarvis** to replace the existing sheet name. Press the Enter key to fix the new name in place.

6 Select Sheet1 (2). Delete the input data and prepare an invoice for another customer as shown in Figure 6.3.

Avondale Computers

	Customer				Order no		299
Name	P Hunt						
Address	12 Sackville Street				**Date**		12/09/02
	Bristol						
	BS2 6GB				**Time**		3:30 PM
Phone							

Code	Item description	Unit price		Number		Cost	
B128	Lexmark E210 printer	£	170.00	1	£	170.00	
C25	Colour ink cartridge	£	25.99	1	£	25.99	
C26	Black ink cartridge	£	15.99	2	£	31.98	
B452	Epson Perfection 2450 scanner	£	263.00	1	£	263.00	

					Subtotal	£	490.97
					Carriage	£	5.00
					Total	£	495.97

Figure 6.3 Invoice for P Hunt

7 Rename the sheet from Sheet1 (2) to **Hunt**.

8 Create another copy of the invoice sheet. Change the data so that the invoice is addressed to yourself, with order number 300. Choose your own date, time and order details.

9 Rename this new sheet, giving it your own surname.

10 Save the workbook.

> **Hint:**
>
> If you have trouble deleting or editing the invoice, the cells may be locked. Remove protection from the sheet and unlock the cells you need to change. Put protection back on again.

Task 6.3 — Move worksheets within a workbook

It might be useful to arrange the worksheets in alphabetical order of the customer's name. You can move a worksheet using the Move or Copy dialogue box that you saw before, but there is a quicker way.

> **Hint:**
>
> Using the Move or Copy dialogue, you can move a worksheet to a different workbook.

Method

1 Point your mouse to the Jarvis sheet tab. Hold down the left mouse button and drag to the right. Let go of the mouse button and drop the Jarvis sheet when it is to the right of the Hunt sheet.

2 Move the worksheet with your name into place in the same way.

Task 6.4   Edit and print selected worksheets

Method

1   Unprotect each of the sheets so that you will be able to make changes to cells that you have not unlocked. You have to unprotect each sheet individually. You cannot unprotect them all at the same time.
2   Hold down the Ctrl key as you click each worksheet tab in turn. All three tabs should be white, showing that the sheets are selected. It does not matter which sheet is in front.
3   Go to cell B20 and key in **Payment due within 30 days**. Remember to press Enter.
4   Select each sheet in turn. You should find that the text has been entered on all three sheets.
5   Select all three sheets again. Click on the View menu and select Header and Footer.
6   Put your name in a header. In the footer, put the date on the left, the file name and sheet name in the centre and the page number on the right.
7   All three sheets should still be selected. Print preview. You should find that there are three pages, numbered 1, 2 and 3. There is one page for each sheet.
8   Print. All three sheets should print out.
9   Save the workbook.

Hint:

If you print each sheet separately, all three sheets will be numbered as page 1. To show consecutive page numbers you have to print them all together.

Task 6.5   Copy from one sheet to another without links

You have learned to copy complete sheets, but you can also copy data from one sheet to another. You can copy contents only, formats only or both contents and formats.

Method

1   Insert a new blank worksheet into your Avondale2 workbook.
2   Select the Jarvis sheet. Select cells A1 to G23 and give the copy command.
3   Select the new worksheet, select cell A1 and give the paste command.
4   You should find that the contents and formats of the cells are pasted into the new sheet. The only difference is that the cell widths are not copied to the new sheet.
5   Click the Undo button on the toolbar or click the Edit menu and select Undo Paste. This reverses your last action and removes the data you pasted.
6   Check that the cells on the Jarvis sheet are still selected and have the dotted marquee round them. If not, select them and give the copy command again.

Hint:

When you paste, a small icon with the Paste symbol appears at the bottom right of the range of cells you pasted. Point the mouse to the icon. An arrow appears. Click it to see a drop down list of options. One of the options is 'Keep source column widths'. If you click this option, the column widths will be adjusted.

7 Select cell A1 on the new sheet. Click the Edit menu and select Paste Special from the drop down list. The Paste Special dialogue box should appear.

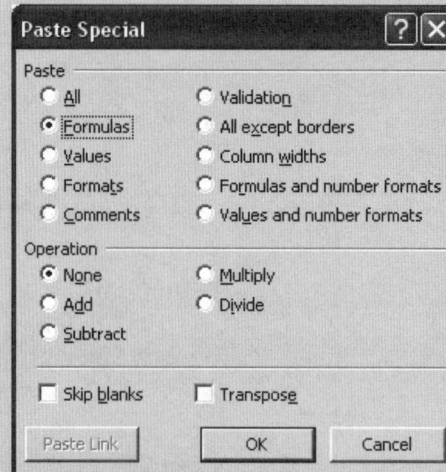

Figure 6.4 The Paste Special dialogue box

8 The default is to paste all. This would be the same as giving the normal paste command. Select the Formulas option and click OK.

9 You should find that the cell contents are pasted but the formats are not. The formulas have been copied. Click into cell F13 and into other cells containing formulas to check that the formulas have been pasted in.

10 Undo the paste.

11 Paste Special again, but this time choose the Formats option. You should find that the formats are pasted but the cell contents are not. You can see any borders and coloured fills. Try keying in data to cells F6, F8 and D13 to show that the number formatting to date, time or currency has been pasted in too.

Task 6.6	Copy values only to make a summary

You will make a sheet to summarise data from the invoices.

Method

1 Insert a new worksheet and rename it. Call it **Summary1**.

2 Enter a title and headings as shown in Figure 6.5.

	A	B	C	D
1	**Avondale Computers Invoice Summary 1**			
2				
3	Name		Order No	Date	Total
4				

Figure 6.5 Summary Sheet 1

3 Select cell C5 of the Hunt sheet and copy it. Paste into cell A4 of the summary sheet. You should now have the name P Hunt on the summary sheet.

4   Copy the order number and date from the Hunt sheet and paste them into the summary sheet.

5   Next you need to copy the total from the Hunt sheet, but there is a problem. Try it anyway. Copy the total from cell F20 of the Hunt sheet and paste into cell D4 of the summary sheet. The formula is pasted in. It has relative references so it alters to =D2+D3. There are no numbers in cells D2 or D3 so an error message is displayed.

6   Rather than paste in a formula, you need to paste in the value £495.97 that is the result of the formula. Try again. This time, use Paste Special instead of ordinary Paste, and select Values from the Paste Special dialogue box. The value of the result is pasted in instead of the formula itself.

7   Copy and paste the data from the other two invoices in the same way. Use Paste Special Values to paste in the totals.

8   Go to cell D7 of the summary sheet and put in a formula to find the total of the invoices to all three customers.

9   Save the workbook.

Task 6.7 — Copy with a link

The data in your existing summary sheet is not linked in any way to the original data in the invoices. If you change the invoices, the data in the summary will not change. Next you will make a summary with data that is linked to the original invoices. You can create a link by using a variation of copy and paste, or you can enter a formula directly into a cell.

Method using copy and paste link

1   Insert a new worksheet into your workbook. This worksheet should be called **Summary2**.

2   Enter a title and headings just as you did for the Summary1 sheet. This time the heading should say Summary 2 instead of Summary1.

3   Click on the tab of the Hunt sheet then click in cell C5. Cell C5 should contain the name P Hunt. Give the copy command.

4   Go to cell A4 of your Summary2 sheet. Click on the Edit menu and select Paste Special from the drop down list.

5   Click the Paste Link button in the dialogue box. The name P Hunt should appear in cell A4. Look at the formula bar, and you should see that cell A4 now contains the formula =Hunt!$C$5. This is a reference to cell C5 on the Hunt sheet, the cell that contains the information you chose to copy. The exclamation mark is used at the end of the sheet name. There is now a link between the cells. If you change the contents of cell C5 on the Hunt sheet then the display in cell A4 of the Summary2 sheet will change too. The link is one way only. If you enter something else in cell A4 of the Summary2 sheet then you will break the link.

6   Copy cell F4 of the Hunt sheet. Use Paste Link to paste into cell B4 of your Summary2 sheet.

Hint:

The little Paste icon with its drop down list includes options for pasting values only and pasting with a link.

7 Copy cell F6 of the Hunt sheet. Use Paste Link to paste into cell C4 of your Summary2 sheet.

8 Copy cell F20 of the Hunt sheet. Use Paste Link to paste into cell D4 of your Summary2 sheet. You now have the summary information for customer P Hunt. All the summary information is linked back to the original data on the Hunt sheet.

Method using direct entry of a formula

Paste Link puts in a formula giving a reference to the cell you want to copy. You can put the formula in yourself without using Paste Link. You will now copy information from the Jarvis sheet to the summary sheet.

1 Go to cell A5 of the Summary2 sheet. Start to enter a formula. Key in the = sign but do not press Enter yet.

2 Click on the tab of the Jarvis sheet, then click in cell C5. Press the Enter key.

3 The name J K Jarvis should appear in cell A5. Look at the formula bar, and you should see that cell A5 now contains the formula =Jarvis!C5.

4 Continue putting in formulas until the information from all three sheets is displayed. You can either use Copy and Paste Link, or you can enter the formulas directly.

5 Go to cell D7 of the Summary2 sheet and put in a formula to find the total of the invoices to all three customers.

6 Your Summary2 sheet should now display exactly the same data as your Summary1 sheet. Check to make sure that this is the case.

7 Save the workbook.

8 Select the Hunt sheet and change the number of black ink cartridges to 4. The invoice total changes to £527.95.

9 Look at your Summary1 sheet. The total for Hunt should still be £495.95.

10 Look at your Summary2 sheet. The total for Hunt should have changed to £527.95, the same as the total on the altered invoice. The final total should also have changed.

11 Save the workbook.

Hint:

You could key in the formula = Jarvis!C5, but it is probably easier to put the cell reference in the formula by selecting the cell.

Hint:

When you used Paste Link, the linking formula used an absolute reference, e.g. Jarvis!$C$5. When you enter a formula yourself, it uses a relative reference, e.g. Hunt!C5, unless you deliberately change the reference to make it absolute. Does it matter? Only if you copy the linking formula to another cell. As usual, absolute references will not change but relative references will change to suit the new location.

Information: Copying, copying values only and linking

You have tried out a variety of methods of copying from one worksheet to another. When you copy and paste, you can choose to paste cell contents including formulas and formatting. You can paste contents without formatting or formatting without contents. You can paste values only when you want the results of formulas but not the formulas themselves. When you use copy and paste there is normally no link between the original data and the copy. If you want to keep a link between the original data and the copy, you do it by using a formula to link the cells. Changes in the original are then reflected in changes in the copy. You can link either by using copy and paste link or by entering a linking formula directly. →

Should you copy and paste, or should you link? It depends on what you need the spreadsheet to do. Sometimes you want a copy that does not change. You might want to know what the values were at a certain fixed time. Sometimes you want a linked copy that does change so that it always shows the most up-to-date data.

All these copy, paste and link methods work for copying within a sheet as well as from one sheet to another. They also work between one workbook and another. There are some extra things to consider when you link from one workbook to another, because workbooks are saved in separate files. If you delete a workbook or move one of the workbooks to a different folder then you will break the link. Linked workbooks should be kept in the same folder, and they usually have names that show they are related.

Task 6.8   Using more than one workbook

Before you move on to create links between workbooks, you should practise using several workbooks that are open at the same time.

Method

1. Your Avondale2.xls workbook should still be open.
2. Open your Mail Order Clothes.xls workbook.
3. Look at the taskbar at the bottom of the screen. If there are not too many files open, each workbook should have its own button on the taskbar. The buttons show the Excel icon. If a large number of files are open, Windows will group them so that all Excel workbooks share one button. Click a grouped button to see a list of files.

Figure 6.6 Taskbar showing open files and folders

4. One of the buttons on the taskbar looks as if it is pressed in. This is the button belonging to the file or folder that is active and displayed on the screen at the time. Switch from one Excel workbook to the other by clicking on their taskbar buttons.
5. Click on the Window menu to show the drop down list. Your open workbooks should be listed at the bottom of the list. The active workbook should have a tick by its name.
6. Click on the name of the other workbook to make it active. This is an alternative method of switching between open workbooks. It is an older method that was available in earlier versions of Windows and MS Office before files had individual buttons on the taskbar.
7. Click on the Windows menu again. Select Arrange from the drop down list. The Arrange Windows dialogue box appears.
8. Click OK. Both workbooks should be displayed on the screen in their own window.

9	Only one of the workbooks is active at a time. The active workbook has its window title bar shown in brighter blue in the normal Windows colour scheme. Click on the other workbook and it becomes active.
10	Open another Excel workbook so that you have three workbooks open.
11	Click on the Windows menu and select Arrange. Make sure that the Tiled option is selected and click OK.
12	Try out the effects of arranging the workbook windows using the Horizontal, Vertical and Cascade options.
13	Close all workbooks and close down Excel.

Task 6.9   Prepare a folder to hold linked workbooks

You will now prepare a new folder to hold the linked Avondale workbooks that you will create. This will involve some revision of the file and folder management that you learned for Level 1.

Method

1 Click the Start button at the bottom left of the screen. Select My Computer.
2 Select the drive or folder that holds your data files. This may be the My Documents folder at home. If you are using a networked system then you will probably have your own user area on one of the networked drives. If you do not know where your data files are stored then ask your tutor or the person who set up your computer.
3 A window should open showing the files and folders in My Documents or in your network user area.
4 In this window, find and double click on the folder that contains your Excel workbook files. You may have to repeat this action through several layers of folders until you see the files. When you open a new window, the previous window may or may not remain open. It depends on how Windows has been set up on your system. To avoid clutter on the screen it may be a good idea to close any windows that you are not using.

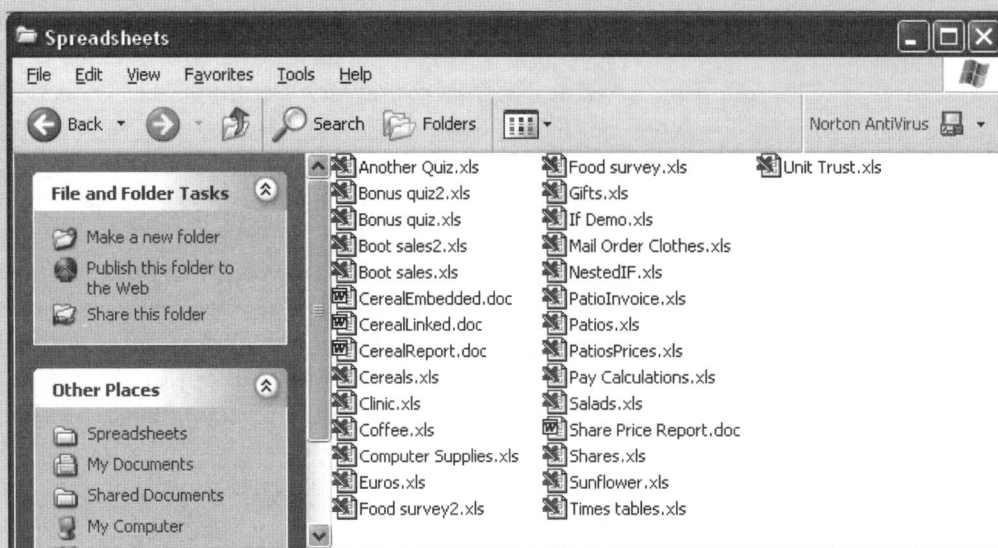

Figure 6.7 Open folder containing Excel workbook files

5   Figure 6.7 shows the files displayed as a list. Your files may be displayed as icons. To change from one kind of display to another, click on the View menu and select from the drop down list. You can select icons, list or details. The display will also differ in different versions of Windows.

6   To create a new folder inside your existing folder, click on the File menu. If you have more than one window displayed, make sure that you use the File menu of the correct window. Select New from the drop down list, then select Folder from the submenu.

7   A new folder should appear in the window, with the name New Folder. Change this name to **Avondale**.

8   Move your two Avondale workbook files to the new Avondale folder. You can use drag and drop, or you can use cut and paste to do this.

9   Check that both files are in the new folder.

Hint:

The older and more general name for a folder is **directory**. A folder within another folder is called a **subdirectory**.

Task 6.10	Copy between workbooks

You will create another summary of the Avondale orders, but this time it will be in a separate workbook. The data will be copied so that it does not change when the original changes.

Method

1   Open your Avondale2.xls workbook file. Click on the tab of the Summary1 sheet to bring it to the front.

2   Create a new Excel workbook and save it into your Avondale folder with the name **Avondale SummaryA.xls**.

3   Arrange the two workbooks vertically so that they appear side by side on the screen.

4   In cell A1 of your new workbook, enter a heading: **Avondale Computers Copied Summary**.

5   Click on the Avondale2 workbook to select it, then select cells A3 to D7 of the Summary1 sheet.

6   Give the copy command.

7   Select cell A3 of your SummaryA workbook. You may need to click twice, once to select the workbook and once more to select the cell.

8   Give the paste command. The headings, data and final total should be pasted into the new workbook. You may need to adjust the widths of some columns to show all the data.

9   Select each cell in turn and check in the formula bar to see the cell contents. You should find that the text (labels) and the numbers (values) have been copied exactly as they were. Cell D7 should contain a formula, copied from cell D7 of the original workbook.

10   There is no link between the workbooks. Go to cell D5 of the Avondale2.xls workbook on the Summary1 sheet. Change the value to £300. The SummaryA workbook is not affected. Change the value back to £255.34.

11   Save the Avondale SummaryA workbook again and close it. Make sure that you have the right workbook selected when you save and close.

Remember:

If a cell shows hash marks ####, it means that the cell is too small to display its contents. Make the cell wider.

You will make another summary workbook, but this time there will be links to the original workbook so that the new workbook changes when the original does. You could make the links from one of the summary sheets in the original workbook, but instead you will make links from the individual invoice sheets.

Method

1   Create a new Excel workbook and save it in the Avondale folder with the name **Avondale SummaryB.xls**.
2   In cell A1 of your new workbook, enter a heading: **Avondale Computers Linked Summary**.
3   Your Avondale2.xls workbook should still be open. Arrange the two workbooks vertically so that they appear side by side on the screen.
4   Enter or copy the headings Name, Order No, Date and Total into cells A3 to D3 of the SummaryB sheet.
5   Select the Avondale2.xls workbook and click on the tab of the Hunt sheet to bring it to the front.
6   Go to cell C5 of the Hunt sheet and give the copy command.
7   Select cell A4 in the SummaryB workbook. Use Edit – Paste Special – Paste Link to put in the formula to make the link between cells. The formula should be =[Avondale2.xls]Hunt!$C$5. It shows the workbook name, the sheet name and the cell reference.
8   You can also enter the formula directly. Go to cell B4 in the SummaryB workbook. Key in the = sign to start the formula.
9   Click into cell F4 of the Hunt sheet. Press Enter to accept the formula =[Avondale2.xls]Hunt!$F$4.
10 Use either method to enter the remaining formulas to make links from the invoice sheets of Avondale2.xls to the new SummaryB workbook.
11 Save the Avondale SummaryB.xls workbook.
12 Go to the Jarvis invoice sheet and change the number of packs of paper to 10. You should see the total on the Jarvis sheet change to £313.26. The total for Jarvis on the linked SummaryB sheet should also change to £313.26.
13 Change the number of packs of paper back to 2. The totals on both sheets should go back to the previous value.

Hint:

Keep linked workbooks together in their own folder. It is easier to set up the folder before you start making links. If you move linked workbook files individually then you are likely to break the links. If you move or copy the whole folder then the links should stay in place between files in the folder.

Information: More copying and moving methods to try

You might like to try out some additional methods of copying data or even whole sheets between workbooks. You can use the Avondale workbooks for your experiments. Close them without saving when you have finished.

You can drag and drop between workbooks when both workbooks are displayed on the screen. Remember that drag and drop by itself will move data. Hold down the Ctrl key as you drag, and the data will be copied. Try dragging data to a cell in another workbook.   →

You can drag and drop whole worksheets. Use the worksheet tag to drag a worksheet into a different workbook. Again, you hold down the Ctrl key if you want to make a copy.

Right click on a worksheet tab. Select Move or Copy from the pop-up menu. Using the dialogue box, you can move or copy the sheet to a different open workbook, or to a new workbook.

Task 6.12 — Copy a chart from one workbook to another, keeping a link

You can copy a chart from one workbook to another. A chart is linked to its source data. When you copy a chart to another workbook, it still needs to remain linked to its source data.

Method

1 Create a new folder to contain your Exports workbooks. Give the new folder the name **Exports**. Move your Exports.xls and Exports2.xls workbooks to this folder.

2 Open your Exports.xls workbook. Select the worksheet that shows the original data. There should also be a chart on this sheet. If not, then create a pie chart to show the exports in 1998 and put it on the sheet with the data.

3 Save any changes you have made to the Exports.xls workbook.

4 Create a new workbook and save it as **ExportLink.xls**. Put it in the Exports folder with your Exports.xls workbook.

5 Arrange both workbooks side by side on the screen.

6 Select the chart on the worksheet in your Exports.xls workbook. The black resize handles should appear in the corners and in the middle of the sides of the chart area.

7 Give the copy command.

8 Select the new ExportLink.xls workbook. Give the paste command. A copy of the chart is pasted into the new workbook. You can move this new chart and resize it on its worksheet.

9 Select the original Exports.xls workbook. Change the data for the USA for 1998 to 25. Both charts should change to show the new percentages.

10 Change the data back to 12.4. You should be able to use the Undo button to do this. Both charts change back. The new chart is linked to the original data.

11 You might like to try changing the formatting of the charts. You can change the fonts, the colours, etc. The charts are independent of each other in their formatting. The data values are shared.

12 Save the ExportLink.xls workbook.

13 Select the Exports.xls workbook and click on the tab of its Column Chart Year 1 sheet to select it. You should see the column chart on the screen.

14 Right click on the tab of the Column Chart Year 1 sheet and select Move or Copy from the pop-up menu.

15	Click to place a tick in the Create a Copy check box. Click on the arrow to open the drop down list labelled 'To Book'. Select ExportLink.xls from the list. Click OK.
16	A copy of the column chart should appear on its own sheet in the ExportLink.xls workbook.
17	Check that the copy of the column chart is linked to its original data by changing the data for the USA for 1998 to 25. The chart should change to show the new value. Change the data back to 12.4.
18	Save the ExportLink.xls workbook and close it.

Task 6.13 Copy a picture of a chart between workbooks

If you want to copy a chart to another workbook but not leave a link, then you cannot copy the chart directly, but you can copy a picture of the chart.

Method

1	Your Exports.xls workbook should still be open. Select the worksheet that contains the original data as well as a chart.
2	Create a new workbook and save it as **ExportCopy.xls**. Put it in the **Exports** folder with your Exports.xls workbook.
3	Arrange both workbooks side by side on the screen.
4	Select the chart on the sheet in the Exports.xls workbook so that its resize handles appear.
5	Hold down the Shift key on the keyboard as you click on the Edit menu.
6	Select Copy Picture from the drop down list. This option does not appear unless you use the Shift key.
7	The Copy Picture dialogue box appears.

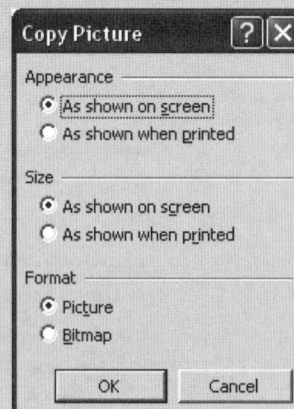

Figure 6.8 The Copy Picture dialogue box

8	In the Appearance section, select 'As shown on screen'. Size should be 'As shown on screen'. Format should be 'Picture'. Click OK.
9	Select the ExportCopy.xls workbook.
10	Give the paste command.
11	A picture of the chart appears on the worksheet. It looks just like the original chart, but it is not linked to the original data.

12 To test that there is no link, change the data for the USA for 1998 to 25, then change it back to 12.4. The picture of the chart should not change.

13 The picture does not behave like a normal chart. You cannot select individual sections of the picture for formatting. It is just like a snapshot taken of the chart.

14 Save the ExportCopy.xls worksheet and close it.

| Task 6.14 | Use hyperlinks |

Hyperlinks are not included in the City & Guilds outcomes for Level 2, but they are included here because they can be helpful when navigating between workbooks.

Method

1 Open your Exports.xls workbook and select the worksheet that contains the original data.

2 Select cell B2, which should be empty.

3 Click on the Insert menu and select Hyperlink from the drop down list. The Insert Hyperlink dialogue box appears.

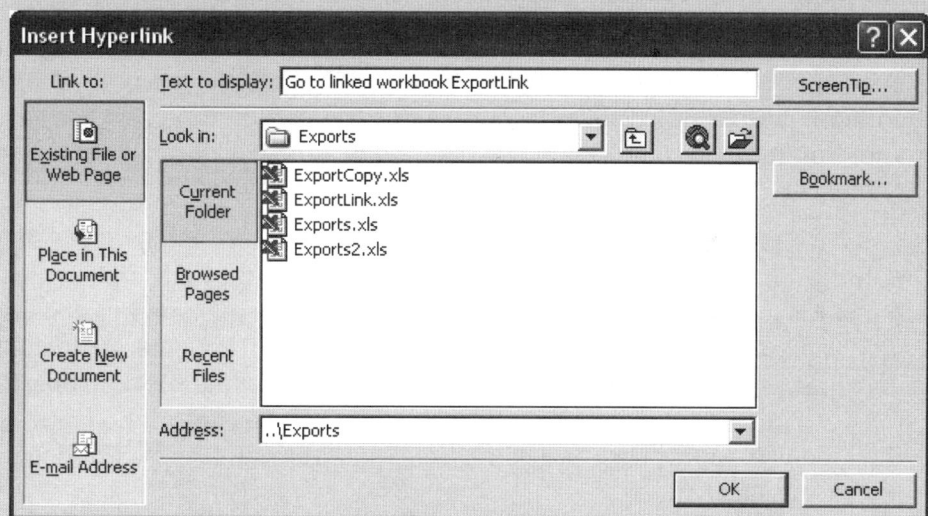

Figure 6.9 Insert Hyperlink dialogue box

4 There are four large buttons on the left of the dialogue box. The top button, 'Existing File or Web Page', should be selected by default.

5 Click into the white text box at the top of the dialogue box, labelled 'Text to display'. Key in **Go to linked workbook ExportLink**. This is the text that the computer user will see.

6 Inspect the central part of the window. It is a bit like the Open File dialogue box.

7 In the central part of the window, find and select your ExportLink.xls workbook.

8 The path and file name ExportLink.xls should now appear in the white box labelled 'Address'. It may be too long to show fully.

9 Click OK.

Hint:

You can hyperlink to a specific sheet, cell or named range within a workbook by using the 'Place in this document' button in the Insert Hyperlink dialogue box. You can hyperlink to other types of file on your computer, not just Excel files. If you have an Internet connection, you can hyperlink to a web site. You might like to experiment if you have time.

10 Cell B2 of your worksheet should now display the text 'Go to linked workbook ExportLink'. The text should be blue and underlined to show that it is a hyperlink.
11 Point the mouse at cell B2. The mouse pointer should change to a hand with a pointing finger. A yellow label should appear showing the path to the ExportLink file.
12 Click on cell B2. The ExportLink.xls workbook should open.
13 Save Exports.xls. Close both workbooks. Close down Excel.

Information: Importing and extracting data

It is often useful to be able to import data into a spreadsheet or to extract data out of a spreadsheet. Suppose you have a spreadsheet showing sales information for February. You might want to import data on prices. You might want to export calculated totals or profit figures to a summary spreadsheet for the year. Importing and extracting data saves a lot of extra keying in.

Another advantage of importing or extracting data is the ability to link data in cells so that you can change the original data and all the copies will change too. You need only make each change once. It helps to keep all the data consistent.

Sometimes you will not want to link data. The copy may show a value at a given time, and you do not want the copy to change to show the current value.

You have learned several methods of importing or extracting data from one sheet to another or from one workbook to another. Excel's copy and paste facilities are quite flexible. You can paste cell contents, values or formats without making a link. You can paste with a link. You can use the drag and drop method to move or copy data. You can make a link by keying in a formula with a cell reference.

You have also learned how to copy a chart from one workbook to another. You can copy and paste, keeping a link to the original data, or you can copy and paste a picture of the chart that is not linked. A chart is just one example of an object that can be copied and pasted. There are other objects that you have not used in your Level 2 spreadsheet work. These objects include clipart pictures, shapes or drawings, control buttons, sound files, video clips and more. Some objects can be copied with a link to the original and some cannot. Some objects can be copied and embedded in the spreadsheet so that you can double click and edit them. Some cannot be edited. It depends on the type of object and how it was created.

The City & Guilds criteria ask you to identify the differences between copying data values, linking data values and pasting data objects. In this section, you have carried out tasks involving copying and pasting data without links, linking data, and copying and pasting chart objects.

When you have a large number of spreadsheet workbooks, it is important to keep them well organised so that you can easily find the one you need. All workbooks should have descriptive names that indicate their contents. Different versions of a workbook should have names that indicate the version as well as the contents. Linked workbooks should have names that show they are related.

Folders (directories) should be used to keep workbooks organised. Related workbooks should be kept together, perhaps in a special folder of their own. In particular, linked workbooks should be kept together. Beware of deleting or moving linked workbooks. If you delete or move one without the other(s) then you will leave broken links.

→ Practise your skills 6.1: Swimming club spreadsheets

You will create a set of linked worksheets and workbooks to display and analyse the finances of the Swim-fit Swimming Club. The club hires the pool at the Avondale Leisure Centre for one session a week. Members pay an annual joining fee. They also pay a fee for each session they attend. The club sells a range of equipment in order to make money.

1 Create a new folder inside the folder where you normally save Excel workbook files. Give your new folder the name **Swimming**.

2 Load Excel.

3 Create a new spreadsheet and save it in your Swimming folder with the name **SwimQuarterly.xls**.

4 Enter data as shown in Figure 6.10. Cells F7 to F11 and cells F16 to F18 should contain formulas to find the totals for each type of income or outgoing. Cells C12 to E12 and cells C19 to E19 should contain formulas to find the total income or outgoing for each month.

5 Format the spreadsheet as shown. Use bold font, font size, alignment, borders and shading to create the effect.

	B	C	D	E	F
Swim-fit Swimming Club					
Avondale Leisure Centre					
Income	**2001**				
		Jan	**Feb**	**Mar**	**Quarterly Total**
Joining fees		400	200	195	795
Session fees		50	95	115	260
Donations		35	0	19	54
Sales		270	220	150	640
Other		25	35	40	100
Total		**780**	**550**	**519**	
Outgoings					
		Jan	**Feb**	**Mar**	**Quarterly total**
Pool hire		500	500	500	1500
Stock		100	50	0	150
Admin		55	28	32	115
Total		**655**	**578**	**532**	

Figure 6.10 Swimming club spreadsheet for Quarter 1

6 Unlock cells C7 to E11 and cells C16 to E18. These cells contain input data.

7 Right click on the sheet tab, select Rename, and give the sheet the name **Quarter1**.

8 Protect the sheet. Save the workbook.

9 Select cells A1 to G20. Copy these cells and paste them to Sheet2, starting in cell A1. Adjust column widths on Sheet2 to match the original widths. (You can use Paste Special to paste column widths, or use the little Paste icon's drop down menu.)

10 Rename Sheet2. Give it the name **Quarter2**.

11 On the Quarter2 sheet, change the month names in rows 6 and 15 to Apr, May, Jun.

12 Unlock the data input cells. Protect the Quarter2 sheet.

13 Delete the values in cells C7 to E11 and cells C16 to E18. Check that all formulas are still in place and showing zero results.

14 Save the workbook.

15 Prepare two more worksheets in the same way. A **Quarter3** sheet should be ready to hold data for July, August and September. A **Quarter4** sheet should be ready to hold data for October, November and December.

16 Enter data into your worksheets for Quarters 2, 3 and 4. Select the data from Table 6.1. Check the results of the formulas.

17 Save the workbook.

	Apr	May	Jun	Jul	Aug	Sep	Oct	Nov	Dec
Income									
Joining fees	220	150	340	120	150	50	280	150	50
Session fees	100	120	400	580	650	420	320	120	120
Donations	0	0	25	0	0	0	10	0	50
Sales	220	100	250	450	230	120	70	100	350
Other	10	0	0	0	25	0	0	30	45
Outgoings									
Pool hire	500	500	500	500	500	500	500	500	500
Stock	50	100	100	100	200	100	0	50	50
Admin	20	14	25	12	20	32	25	21	30

Table 6.1 Data for the quarterly Swimming worksheets

18 Insert a new worksheet into the workbook. Move the new worksheet to the end, after Quarter4. Rename the new worksheet as **IncomeChart**.

19 Enter labels into the new worksheet as shown in Figure 6.11.

	A	B	C	D	E
1	**Swim-fit Swimming Club**				
2	Income				
3					
4		Quarter1	Quarter2	Quarter3	Quarter4
5	Joining fees				
6	Session fees				
7	Donations				
8	Sales				
9	Other				

Figure 6.11 The IncomeChart worksheet

20 Copy the quarterly totals for income from the Quarter1 sheet. Paste them, values only, into the IncomeChart worksheet, starting in cell B5. (You are pasting the results of the formulas but not the formulas themselves. There is no link to the original results.)

21 Copy the quarterly totals for income from the Quarter2, Quarter3 and Quarter4 sheets and paste them, values only, into the appropriate columns of the IncomeChart sheet.

22 Save the workbook.

23 Create a column chart using the data on the IncomeChart sheet. Sources of income should be used as X axis labels, and the legend should show the quarters. Add suitable titles. Place the chart on the same sheet as the data.

24 Save the workbook. This workbook is now complete. Leave it open.

25 Create a new Excel workbook. Save it in your Swimming folder with the name **Swim2001.xls**. →

26 Start entering data as shown in Figure 6.12. In row 6, continue the month names to December. (Use the fill handle to fill month names.)

	A	B	C	D	E	F	G
1	**Swim-fit Swimming Club**						
2	**Avondale Leisure Centre**						
3							
4	Balance from 2000		1047				
5							
6		Jan	Feb	Mar	Apr	May	Jun
7	Income						
8	Outgoings						
9	Balance						

Figure 6.12 Starting the Swim2001 spreadsheet

27 In cell B7, put a formula that will make a link to cell C12 of the Quarter1 sheet of the SwimQuarterly workbook. This formula will display the total income figure for January. You can put in this formula directly or by using copy and paste link. The formula should be: =[SwimQuarterly.xls]Quarter1!$C$12

28 In cell B8, put a formula to make a link with cell C19 of the Quarter1 sheet of the SwimQuarterly workbook. The total outgoings figure for January should now be displayed in cell B8.

29 Continue entering formulas to make links to cells in the SwimQuarterly workbook until the income and outgoings figures are displayed for each month, January to December.

30 In cell B9, enter a formula that will take the balance from the year 2000, add the January income and subtract the January outgoings.

31 In cell C9, enter a formula that will take the balance from January, add the February income and subtract the February outgoings.

32 Replicate the formula to find the balance for each of the other months.

33 Save the workbook.

34 Copy the chart from the IncomeChart sheet of your SwimQuarterly workbook to Sheet2 of your Swim2000 workbook.

35 Save and close both workbooks.

→ Check your knowledge

Answer the questions without using a real spreadsheet.

1 In a spreadsheet, cell A1 contains 3 and cell A2 contains 2. Cell A3 contains =A1+A2. You copy cells A1 to A3, click into cell C1 and click the Paste toolbar button. What does cell C3 contain, and what does it display?

2 You edit cell A2 so that it contains 6. What does cell C3 display now?

3 You edit cell C2 so that it contains 4. What does cell C3 display now?

4 Cell A1 contains 3 and cell A2 contains 2. Cell A3 contains =A1+A2. You copy cells A1 to A3, click into cell D1 and then click Edit, Paste Special, choose Values and click OK. What does cell D3 contain, and what does it display?

5 You edit cell D2 so that it contains 4. What does cell D3 display now?

6 Cell A1 contains 3 and cell A2 contains 2. Cell A3 contains =A1+A2. You copy cells A1 to A3, click into cell E1 and then click Edit, Paste Special, then click Paste Link. What does cell E3 contain, and what does it display?

7 You edit cell A2 so that it contains 6. What does cell E3 display now?

8 You can move cell contents using the drag and drop method. How do you use drag and drop to copy?

You will learn to

- Set margins
- Fit a spreadsheet on one page
- Set page size and orientation
- Adjust page breaks
- Print a selected area of a spreadsheet
- Print in monochrome or colour
- Specify the printouts required from a spreadsheet

Information: Printing options

You have learned a range of techniques that you can use to prepare a spreadsheet and display it effectively on the screen. In this section you will explore printing options in more detail. Many of the options may already be familiar. When you first design a spreadsheet, you should decide what printouts will be needed and write the details of the printing options into your design.

Task 7.1 Set up a demonstration spreadsheet

You will set up a spreadsheet to display a summary of the accident record of a company. This spreadsheet can then be used to explore printing options.

Method

1. Start Excel and create a new workbook called **Accidents.xls**.
2. Enter data as shown in Figure 7.1.

	A	B	C	D	E	F	G
1		Accidents					
2							
3		North region in year:			South region in year:		
4		1999	2000	2001	1999	2000	2001
5	Severe injury	6	4	5	8	9	2
6	Loss of time, not severe	13	24	16	22	31	18
7	Minor injury, no loss of time	24	31	26	40	51	22
8	Property damage only	41	32	34	41	60	42
9	Near miss	179	150	142	166	204	120
10	Total						

Figure 7.1 Accidents spreadsheet

3. Enter formulas to find a total for each column.
4. Use borders as shown. There are outline and inner borders round cells A5 to G10 and B3 to G4. In addition there are heavier outline borders round cells B3 to D9, B10 to D10, E3 to G9 and E10 to G10.

5   The heading Accidents is centred in cell C1. Do not merge the cells in row 1 or use 'Centre across selection'. This would give problems later.
6   Increase the widths of columns B, C, D, E, F and G to 11.
7   Save the workbook.

| Task 7.2 | Explore printing options: margins |

You will change the margins directly in Print Preview and by using the Page Setup dialogue box. Margins control the amount of white (empty) space between the edge of the paper and the printed material. You can use margins to improve the display. You can also make margins smaller to fit more on a page, but if you make margins too small your spreadsheet may not print properly.

Method

1   Print preview. By default, you should find that the spreadsheet needs two sheets of paper in portrait orientation.
2   Click the Margins button at the top of the Print Preview window. Lines appear showing the positions of the margins.

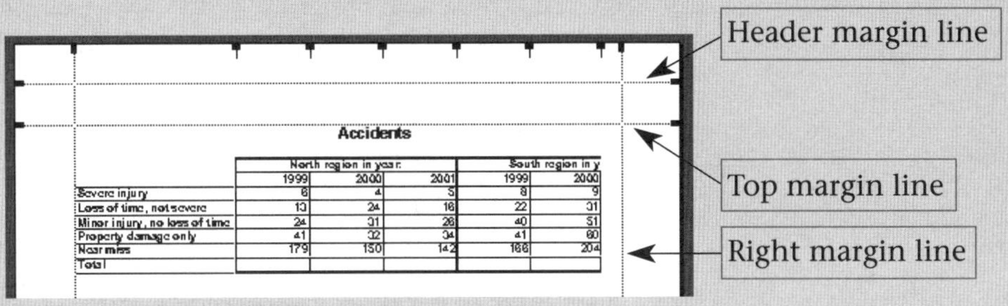

Figure 7.2 Part of Print Preview showing margins

3   Identify the lines showing the left and right margins, the top and bottom margins and the header and footer margins. If there is a header, it will display between the header margin and the top margin. There are also marks at the top of the display to show the column widths.
4   Margins and column widths can be changed in this view. Point the mouse to the black mark where a margin line meets the edge of the paper. The mouse pointer should change to a line with a double-headed arrow. You can drag the mouse to change the margin.
5   Try making the left and right margins smaller. Can you fit the whole spreadsheet on one page? Make the left and right margins larger.
6   Make the top margin bigger so that the spreadsheet moves down the page. You could also change the header margin.
7   Click the Setup button at the top of the Print Preview window. The Page Setup dialogue box appears. You can also reach this dialogue box from the normal spreadsheet view by clicking on the File menu and selecting Page Setup.
8   Click on the Margins tab in the dialogue box to bring the Margins section to the front.

9   You can set margins either by keying in the values you want or by clicking on the little up and down arrows beside the input boxes. Set the top and bottom margins to 2.5, which was their original default value. Set the right and left margins to 1.9. Set the header and footer margins to 1.3.
10   Click OK and watch the margins change on the Print Preview.
11   Click on the Setup button to show the Page Setup dialogue box again.
12   Click the check boxes to centre the spreadsheet horizontally and vertically on the page. Click OK and see the effect.
13   Show the Page Setup dialogue again. Click to remove the ticks from the check boxes and click OK. The spreadsheet goes back to its former position on the page.

| Task 7.3 | Explore printing options: fit on a page, orientation and paper size |

If a spreadsheet is slightly too wide to fit on one page there are various ways you can make it fit. If it is in portrait orientation you might be able to change to landscape. You could change the margins. You could make columns narrower, even changing font sizes if necessary, though this will also affect the display on the screen which may be a bad idea. A better way of fitting a spreadsheet on one page may be to use Excel's own built-in methods.

In the UK we normally print on A4 paper. It may be possible for you to use different sizes of paper. This will depend on your printer and the way your system has been set up.

Method

1   Start with your spreadsheet displayed in Print Preview as before.
2   Show the Page Setup dialogue box. Click on the Page tab to bring the Page section to the front.

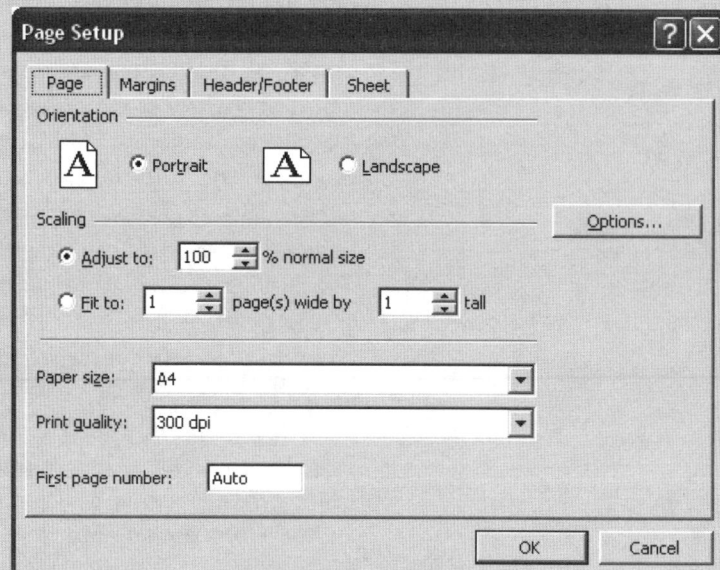

Figure 7.3 Page section of the Page Setup dialogue box

3   You have a choice of portrait or landscape orientation. This should already be familiar.

4   The scaling options give you two ways of scaling the spreadsheet for printing. The default is 'Adjust to 100% normal size'. Change 100 to 75. Click OK.

5   Look at the effect in Print Preview. The spreadsheet is scaled down to a smaller size for printing, but the normal screen display would not be affected. Check this by closing Print Preview so that you see the normal spreadsheet view.

6   Print preview again. Show the Page Setup dialogue box.

7   Click in the 'Fit to' option button so that you have selected 'Fit to 1 page(s) wide by 1 page(s) tall'. Click OK.

8   Print Preview shows that the spreadsheet has been scaled to fit exactly on one page. Again, the normal spreadsheet view is not changed.

9   Show the Page Setup dialogue box again. Click in the 'Adjust to' option button and change to 100% normal size.

10   Click the arrow at the right of the 'Paper size' box to see what options are listed. These may include Letter, which is a US size fairly close to A4 size. There may be A5 size and various envelope sizes. Select A4 size.

11   Notice that there is an option to set the first page number. You do not have to start with 1. Click OK to close the dialogue box and keep changes.

12   Close Print Preview.

Task 7.4   Explore printing options: set and adjust page breaks

Excel automatically puts in page breaks where there is no space to continue on one page and it is necessary to start another. These automatic page breaks are called soft page breaks. You can insert page breaks at positions that you choose. These page breaks deliberately inserted by the user are called hard page breaks. The idea of hard and soft page breaks may be familiar from word processing.

Method

1   Start with your spreadsheet on the screen in the normal view. There is probably a faint dotted line between columns F and G, showing that there is an automatic page break there. If no line shows, check that you set the scaling option back to 'Adjust to 100% normal size' near the end of Task 7.3.

2   Select cell E1.

3   Click on the Insert menu and select 'Page Break'. A slightly darker dotted line should appear between columns D and E. The original page break line should disappear. An automatic page break is no longer needed after column F.

4   Print preview and check that the spreadsheet would print on two pages with a break after column D. Close Print Preview.

5   Select cell E1.

6   Click on the Insert menu and select Remove Page Break. The hard page break line should disappear and the soft page break line between columns F and G should reappear.

7 Select cell E7.

8 Click on the Insert menu and select 'Page Break'. This time there should be a break between columns D and E as before, but there should also be a break between rows 6 and 7. The line between the rows may be hard to see. Check in Print Preview that there are now four pages.

9 Click on the View menu and select Page Break Preview from the drop down list. You may see a message as the Page Break Preview opens. This welcome message tells you that you can adjust the page breaks by clicking and dragging with the mouse. Click OK to close the message box.

	A	B	C	D	E	F	G
1		Accidents					
2							
3		North region in year:			South region in year:		
4		1999	2000	2001	1999	2000	2001
5	Severe injury	6	4	5	8	9	2
6	Loss of time, not severe	13	24	16	22	31	18
7	Minor injury, no loss of time	24	31	26	40	51	22
8	Property damage only	41	32	34	41	60	42
9	Near miss	179	150	142	166	204	120
10	Total	2262	2241	2224	2276	2355	2205

Figure 7.4 Page Break Preview

10 Page Break Preview shows the positions of the page breaks and it also shows the page numbers in grey on the pages.

11 Point the mouse at the page break line between rows 6 and 7. The mouse pointer should change to a double-headed arrow. Drag the line down until it is between rows 10 and 11, in the same place as the bottom page break line. You should now have only two pages.

12 Point the mouse at the page break line between columns D and E. Drag it to between columns E and F. Check the effect in Print Preview.

13 Go back to normal view of the spreadsheet. If you are in Page Break Preview, then click on the View menu and select Normal from the drop down list. If you are in Print Preview then click on the button labelled Normal view.

Task 7.5   Show and hide objects on a sheet

If a worksheet has an object such as a chart or a picture on it, then normally the object is displayed on the screen and is printed with the sheet. Objects can be hidden if you do not want to display or print them.

Method

1 Create a column chart to show the accident figures for the Northern region in 1999. Place the chart on the worksheet below the data.

2 Click on the Tools menu and select Options from the list. The View tab should be at the front of the Options dialogue box.

3 The Objects section of the window has three option buttons labelled 'Show all', 'Show placeholders' and 'Hide all'. Click on the 'Hide all' option. Click OK.

4 The chart should vanish. Print preview and check that the chart is not shown for printing.

5 Click on the Tools menu and select Options. Click on the 'Show all' option and click OK. The chart appears again.

Task 7.6   Print a selected area of the spreadsheet

The simplest method is to select the area of the spreadsheet and then print the selection. If you want to print the selected area regularly then you can set the print area. Excel will print only this selected area of the sheet until you clear the print area.

Method

1. Start with the normal view of the spreadsheet. Select cells A3 to D10.
2. Click on the File menu and select Print from the drop down list. The Print dialogue box appears. (Do not use the toolbar Print button. It does not show the dialogue box.)
3. In the lower left area of the dialogue box you will find the 'Print what' options. Click in the Selection option button.
4. Click the Preview button in the dialogue box. Only your selected area is shown. Close the Preview.
5. Print preview again starting from the normal view. The whole spreadsheet is previewed. Excel has not 'remembered' the selection.
6. Select cells A3 to D10 again.
7. Click on the File menu and select Print Area, then select Set Print Area from the submenu.
8. Print preview. Only your selected area is shown. Close Print Preview.
9. Print preview again to check that the selection is still shown. Close Print Preview.
10. Click on the File menu and select Print Area, then select Clear Print Area from the submenu.
11. Print preview and check that the whole of the spreadsheet is shown, perhaps on two pages. Close Print Preview.

Task 7.7   Print in monochrome or colour

You may have a colour printer or a black and white printer. If you are working on a network then you may have a choice of printers. It is possible to print in black and white (monochrome) even if you are using a colour printer.

Method

1. Start with your spreadsheet in normal view.
2. Put some colour on your spreadsheet by using formatting options. Give some cells a coloured background and make some of the text coloured.
3. Print preview. You should see the colours in the Preview.

4   If you now print to a colour printer, the printout should appear in colour. Of course, if you only have a black and white printer, your spreadsheet will print in shades of grey.

5   Show the Page Setup dialogue box and click on the Sheet tab.

6   Click in the check box labelled 'Black and white' to place a tick, then click OK. The Preview should now appear in black and white. If you print to a colour printer, the printout should be black and white.

7   Your Page Setup dialogue box also has a button labelled Options. Click this and you should see a dialogue box giving printer setup options. The detail will depend on the make and model of printer you are using. There may be further options for printing in colour or greyscale. There may also be options for printing in high quality, medium quality or draft quality. Close all dialogue boxes you have open.

8   Starting in normal view, click on the File menu and select Print. The Print dialogue box opens.

9   Near the top of the dialogue box is a drop down list labelled 'Name'. Click the arrow to show a list of available printers. On a network, you may have a choice between a colour printer and a black and white printer.

10 While you still have the dialogue box open, notice that you can choose to print chosen pages from a multi-page worksheet. You can also choose to print multiple copies of a sheet. Close the dialogue box.

Task 7.8   Specify the printouts required from a spreadsheet

Method

1   Take a sheet of paper and a pen. Think about the Accidents spreadsheet. On your paper, write down details of the printouts that would be required from the spreadsheet. For each printout, say what size of paper and what orientation it should use. Say whether it will be in colour or monochrome (black and white). Say if it should fit on one page. If more than one page is needed, say where the page break(s) should be. Say whether the printout will be of the whole sheet or of selected cells. Say if you will include gridlines, row numbers and column letters. Say if there are any special requirements such as cells to be repeated on each page. Say what information should be included in the header and footer.

2   Produce your chosen printouts.

Suggested printouts

Two printouts should be sufficient.

I One should be a printout of the whole spreadsheet on A4 paper in normal view. It should fit on one page. You could choose to use landscape orientation or to keep portrait but fit to the page. Monochrome is sufficient but you could print in colour if you wish. It is better not to include gridlines because the cell borders will give a better display without gridlines as well.

2 The second printout should show formulas. It should fit the whole spreadsheet on one sheet of A4 paper. Landscape orientation would be a good choice. Show gridlines, row numbers and column headings so that it is easy to see which cells contain the formulas.

→ ## Practise your skills 7.1: SwimQuarterly spreadsheet

You will produce some printouts using your SwimQuarterly workbook.

1 Open the SwimQuarterly spreadsheet that you created for Practise your skills 6.1. Select the Quarter1 sheet.

2 Print the Quarter1 sheet on one page of A4 paper in portrait orientation. The printout should be centred horizontally and vertically on the page. Gridlines, row numbers and column letters should not be shown. Include a header with your name and a footer with the date, the file name, the sheet name and the page number. If you have a choice between colour and monochrome printing then choose monochrome.

3 Print the Quarter1 sheet showing formulas. It should be on one sheet of A4 paper in portrait orientation. Show the gridlines, row numbers and column letters.

4 Print only the Income section of the Quarter1 sheet, using the normal view showing results. It should not be centred on the page. Use landscape orientation. The left and right margins should be set to 3.5 cm. The top and bottom margins should be set to 4 cm. Adjust the printout to 150% normal size.

5 Save and close the workbook.

Consolidation 2

Scenario

The Environmental Science Information Service has the two workbooks called Carruthers.xls and Jackson.xls that you created for them earlier (Consolidation 1). Now you are asked to create a separate workbook to hold rates of pay. You will also add extra sheets to the existing workbooks and create a workbook to show summary information.

1 Create a new folder (directory) called **Abstracting**. Move your Carruthers.xls and Jackson.xls workbooks to the new folder.

2 Open both workbooks. Change the name of Sheet 1 of each workbook to January. These should be the sheets containing the invoices for four weeks' work in January 2002.

3 Create a new Excel spreadsheet and save it as **RateOfPay.xls** in your Abstracting folder.

4 Copy cells A1 to G8 from your Carruthers.xls workbook January worksheet and paste them into your RateOfPay.xls workbook. Save the workbook.

5 The RateOfPay workbook is now used to hold the master copy of the rates of pay. Copy the rates of pay in cells A5 to A8. Paste them back into the Carruthers.xls workbook, making a link. The original values in the Carruthers.xls workbook should now be replaced with linking formulas. Paste the rates of pay into the Jackson.xls workbook, making a link.

6 Check that changes to the rates of pay in the RateOfPay workbook are reflected in the other workbooks. Restore the rates of pay to their original values.

7 Save all three workbooks.

8 In the Carruthers.xls workbook, copy the complete January spreadsheet and paste it on another sheet in the same workbook. Change the name of this other sheet to February. Enter input data for February as follows.

Batch ref.	Date	Type A	Type B	Type C	Type D
99A005	01/02/02	30	7	0	0
99A006	08/02/02	22	14	0	1
99A007	15/02/02	16	12	1	0
99A008	22/02/02	20	8	0	1

9 Prepare a sheet for March in the same way. Enter data for March.

Batch ref.	Date	Type A	Type B	Type C	Type D
99A009	01/03/02	24	10	0	0
99A010	08/03/02	20	12	0	0
99A011	15/03/02	18	12	2	0
99A012	22/03/02	12	7	0	0
99A013	29/03/02	15	6	0	3

10 Save the workbook.

11 In the Jackson.xls workbook, prepare sheets for February and March. Enter data as follows:

Batch ref.	Date	Type A	Type B	Type C	Type D
02B005	01/02/02	25	6	4	0
02B006	08/02/02	30	3	0	1
02B007	15/02/02	27	14	2	0
02B008	22/02/02	24	12	0	0

Batch ref.	Date	Type A	Type B	Type C	Type D
02B009	01/03/02	22	6	0	0
02B010	08/03/02	13	9	4	0
02B011	15/03/02	30	10	0	0
02B012	22/03/02	16	4	0	0
02B013	29/03/02	12	17	0	2

12 Save the workbook.

13 Create a new workbook and save it with the name **Summary.xls** in the Abstracting folder.

14 Enter titles and labels into the new workbook as shown. The data in cells B5:F6, B10:F11 and B15:F16 should be copied and linked to the totals on the sheets of the Carruthers and Jackson workbooks.

	A	B	C	D	E	F
1	Environmental Science Information Service					
2	Keywords and abstracting by freelance workers					
3						
4	January	Type A	Type B	Type C	Type D	Pay for batch
5	Carruthers	85	37	1	2	£ 66.90
6	Jackson	79	20	0	0	£ 47.60
7	Total					
8						
9	February	Type A	Type B	Type C	Type D	Pay for batch
10	Carruthers	88	41	1	2	£ 71.30
11	Jackson	106	35	6	1	£ 77.00
12	Total					
13						
14	March	Type A	Type B	Type C	Type D	Pay for batch
15	Carruthers	89	47	2	3	£ 78.60
16	Jackson	93	46	4	2	£ 80.00
17	Total					
18						
19	3 Month Total					

Figure 7.5 Summary spreadsheet

15 Enter formulas to find the totals for each month, and to find the totals for the three months. Save the workbook.

16 Add a suitable header and footer, and print the spreadsheet on one sheet of paper. Write Printout 1 on the printout.

17 Print the spreadsheet again showing formulas, gridlines, row numbers and column letters. Write Printout 2 on the printout.

18 Go to the RateOfPay.xls workbook and make some changes. The rate of pay for Type B is now £0.85. The rate of pay for Type D is now £1.30. Save the workbook.

19 Check that the new rates of pay are shown on all sheets of the Carruthers and Jackson workbooks and that the pay has been recalculated. Check that the new totals are shown on the summary sheet.

20 Print the summary sheet again showing the changed totals. Write Printout 3 on the printout.

21 Use the 3 Month Totals to create a pie chart showing the proportions of articles of types A, B, C, D that were processed. Include a title, labels and percentages but do not include a legend.

22 Print the chart on a page of its own with a header and footer. Write Printout 4 on the printout.

23 Create a column chart to show the pay for each person in each month. The data is not arranged on the sheet so that it can easily be selected for this chart. Copy the data, values only, to an empty area of the sheet as shown. Use this copied area to create the chart.

	January	February	March
Carruthers	£ 68.95	£ 73.55	£ 81.25
Jackson	£ 48.60	£ 78.85	£ 82.50

24 Include suitable titles and labels on the axes. Include a legend. Print the chart on a page of its own with a header and footer. Write Printout 5 on the printout.

25 Save the workbook.

26 Close all workbooks and close down Excel.

Section 8 | Spreadsheet design and testing

You will learn to

- Design a spreadsheet on paper to meet a given specification
- Choose test data
- Create a spreadsheet according to your design
- Test the spreadsheet

Information: Designing a spreadsheet to meet a given specification

In your work so far, you have created spreadsheets where the layout is given to you in an illustration. You have usually been told what formulas to use and where to put them. You have also been given step-by-step instructions about formatting and printing. The main part of the design work has been done for you. For Level 2, you need to be able to create a spreadsheet design for yourself to meet a specification provided by a supervisor, colleague or customer.

The design is carried out on paper before you start to use Excel. There may be several sketches giving the overall layout of the spreadsheet and giving details of cell contents, formulas and formatting. The design should allow for the easy input of data. It should include formulas that carry out the required calculations correctly. It should allow the required output data to be easily displayed or printed. You should test the formulas in a spreadsheet before bringing the spreadsheet into use. Part of the design work is planning how the spreadsheet is to be tested, choosing the test data and working out what the results should be.

You have already carried out many of the activities involved in spreadsheet design. In Section 2 you worked on the design of data input forms and saw how they can be improved by suitable choice of formatting. In Section 4 you worked on formulas, the testing of formulas and the choice of test data. In Section 7 you looked at printing options and the choice of printouts. The next task is to put these ideas together and produce a spreadsheet design.

Task 8.1	Produce an initial sketch of a spreadsheet to meet a given specification

Perfect Patios sell building materials for making patios, garden paths and driveways. They sell a variety of paving slabs of different sizes. So that customers can compare the costs of slabs, prices must be given per square metre (m²) as well as per slab. You are asked to prepare a spreadsheet that will calculate the price per square metre for each type of paving slab. (It does not matter if the slabs are not the right size to make an actual square metre of paving. The price per square metre is just a guide to show which slabs will be more expensive than others.)

Here are the length, width and unit costs of each type of slab. Lengths and widths are given in millimetres.

Hamilton paving	600 × 600	slabs cost £ 2.99 each
Hamilton paving	600 × 300	slabs cost £ 1.99 each
Hamilton paving	300 × 300	slabs cost £ 1.49 each
Lindale paving	450 × 450	slabs cost £ 1.49 each
Chiltern paving	400 × 400	slabs cost £ 0.96 each
Derby paving	400 × 400	slabs cost £ 0.90 each

Method

1 Read through the specification and make sure that you understand what is required. We are given the name of each item. We are given the length and width in millimetres. From this we can work out the area of each slab. We are given the cost of one slab. From this we can work out the cost of one square metre of paving. This calculation will be simpler if we show the area of the slab in square metres and not in square millimetres.

2 Make a first sketch of the spreadsheet layout on paper. It might look something like Figure 8.1.

	A	B	C	D	E	F
1	Perfect Patios					
2						
3	Item	Length mm	Width mm	Area m²	Unit price	Price per m²
4	Hamilton paving	600	600		£ 2.99	
5	Hamilton paving	600	300		£ 1.99	
6	Hamilton paving	300	300		£ 1.49	
7	Lindale paving	450	450		£ 1.49	
8	Chiltern paving	400	400		£ 0.96	
9	Derby paving	400	400		£ 0.90	

Figure 8.1 First sketch of the Perfect Patios prices spreadsheet

Task 8.2 Produce a second sketch to show formatting and planned page layout

Method

1 Decide on the formatting to be used and write this on a second sketch. Make a note of cell widths, alignment, font size and enhancement (bold, italic, etc.).

2 Make a note of any borders or background colours you plan to use. Show any cells you plan to unlock before protecting the sheet.

3 Say what size of paper and orientation you will use. Your second sketch might look something like Figure 8.2.

4 Decide if you will need additional data entry forms or special areas for printed reports. These may need extra sketches. As this is a simple spreadsheet, no special data entry form is needed. Data will be entered into the unlocked cells A4 to C9 and E4 to E9. The whole of the spreadsheet will be printed, and there is no need to have a report area elsewhere. It is often a good idea to give a name to ranges that will be printed, so cells A1 to F9 could be named Report.

A width 16 B - F width 10

	A	B	C	D	E	F
1	Perfect Patios					
2						
3	Item	Length mm	Width mm	Area m²	Unit price	Price per m²
4	Hamilton paving	600	600		£ 2.99	
5	Hamilton paving	600	300		£ 1.99	
6	Hamilton paving	300	300		£ 1.49	
7	Lindale paving	450	450		£ 1.49	
8	Chiltern paving	400	400		£ 0.96	
9	Derby paving	400	400		£ 0.90	
10						

A1 Arial size 14 bold

B3:F3 Arial size 10 bold right aligned,

A3:A9 Arial size 10 bold left aligned

B4:D9 Arial size 10 regular, number

E4:F9 Arial size 10 currency 2 decimal places

A3:F9 borders, outline and inside
A4:C9 and E4:E9 unlocked

A4 paper, portrait, centre on sheet

Figure 8.2 Sketch of the Perfect Patio prices spreadsheet showing formats

Task 8.3 Produce a third sketch to show the formulas to be used

Method

1 Make a third sketch and write in the formulas you will use.

2 Add notes if necessary to explain what you are doing. Your third sketch might look something like Figure 8.3.

	A	B	C	D	E	F
1	Perfect Patios					
2						
3	Item	Length mm	Width mm	Area m²	Unit price	Price per m²
4	Hamilton paving	600	600	=B4*C4/1000000	£ 2.99	=E4/D4
5	Hamilton paving	600	300		£ 1.99	
6	Hamilton paving	300	300	Copy down	£ 1.49	Copy down
7	Lindale paving	450	450		£ 1.49	
8	Chiltern paving	400	400		£ 0.96	
9	Derby paving	400	400		£ 0.90	

Figure 8.3 Sketch of the Perfect Patios prices spreadsheet showing formulas

3 The notes could say:
Length * width gives area in mm². Divide by 1,000,000 to give m².
Divide unit price by area to give price per m².
Replicate formulas down to row 9.

Choose test data and calculate the expected results

Method

1 Decide on the data you will use to test the spreadsheet when it is ready. The purpose of testing is to make sure that, given appropriate input data, the spreadsheet will always produce the correct results. It should also check what happens if the input data is not appropriate. You may be told how many sets of test data to use.

As you saw in Section 4, test data often includes representative, marginal, extreme and rogue data. The patio prices spreadsheet will not have any IF functions or any other functions where there is a special marginal value that changes the result. That leaves representative, extreme and rogue data to choose.

2 Work out the expected results yourself on paper. You can use a pocket calculator if you wish.

Representative

Numbers are in the expected range and are chosen to make the calculations easy. All 12 formulas are tested. You could choose test numbers different from those in Table 8.1.

Length mm	Width mm	Area	Unit price	Price per m^2
1000	1000	1	£3.00	£3.00
100	100	0.01	£2.00	£200.00
2000	1000	2	£4.00	£2.00
500	400	0.2	£1.00	£5.00
400	400	0.16	£1.60	£10.00
400	200	0.08	£1.60	£20.00

Table 8.1 Expected results using representative numbers

Extreme

Very large and very small numbers can be chosen as extremes. We expect the spreadsheet to calculate correctly even if the sizes and prices are outside the sensible range for paving stones.

Length mm	Width mm	Area	Unit price	Price per m^2
1000000	200	200	£3.00	£0.01500
200	1000000	200	£2.00	£0.01000
400	400	0.16	£1,000.00	£6,250.00000
1	400	0.0004	£1.00	£2,500.00000
400	1	0.0004	£1.00	£2,500.00000
400	200	0.08	£0.01	£0.12500

Table 8.2 Expected results using extreme numbers

Rogue

Negative numbers or zero would not make sense. What would happen if they are used? What do you expect to happen if entries are not numbers? There is no need to predict the actual error messages that the spreadsheet will display. It is enough to say 'error'.

Length mm	Width mm	Area	Unit price	Price per m^2
0	200	0	£2.00	Can't divide by 0
200	200	0.04	£0.00	£0.00
200	−200	−0.04	£2.00	−£50.00000
200	200	0.04	−£2.00	−£50.00000
aaa	200	error	£2.00	error
200	200	0.04	aaa	error

Table 8.3 Expected results using rogue values

Task 8.5 — Create the spreadsheet according to your design

Method

1 Create a new Excel workbook and save it with the name **PatioPrices.xls.**
2 Enter headings and labels (text) as shown in your sketches. You can enter the numbers too, but these will be replaced later.
3 Format the spreadsheet as shown in your second sketch. This includes unlocking data entry cells as shown in your sketch. Name the Report range.
4 Enter formulas as shown in your third sketch.
5 Add suitable headers and footers.
6 Save the spreadsheet.

Task 8.6 — Modify the design if necessary and record the changes

Method

1 Make any changes that would improve the design. For example, column widths may need to be adjusted.
2 Write down a note of all the changes you make.
3 Protect the spreadsheet.
4 Save the spreadsheet again.

Task 8.7 — Test the spreadsheet

Method

1 Enter the first set of test data.
2 Print the spreadsheet showing the first set of results.
3 Compare the printout with your expected set of results. If the results do not agree then look carefully at the formulas and at your own calculations to work out what went wrong. Make any necessary correction to the formulas until the results agree.
4 Write down what changes you made if any.
5 Enter the second set of test data.
6 Print, check and correct as before.
7 Continue entering data, printing, checking and correcting until you have used all the test data.
8 Save the corrected spreadsheet.
9 Print a copy of the spreadsheet showing formulas.
10 The spreadsheet is now ready for use. Keep all the design sketches, notes and testing records.

Information: Design tips

Input

Certain cells will be used for data entry. Provide clear labels in adjacent cells to show what should be entered. Use formatting to distinguish data entry cells from other cells. Try to design the layout so that all data entry cells are in the same area and visible on the screen at the same time. Unlock data entry cells so that you can protect the sheet and still allow the user to enter data.

Processing

Keep formulas simple if possible. It may be better to split up complicated calculations and do them in stages. If you are going to copy a formula, take care with relative and absolute references. Use named ranges if they help to make the meaning of formulas clearer. Named cells or ranges can be a useful alternative to absolute references. Cells containing formulas should be locked, and the sheet should be protected.

Output

Output can be a screen display or a printout. Use formatting, including borders and background colour, if it helps to make the display clear. You may need to print some of the results rather than the whole spreadsheet. Organise the required results into a report or series of reports for printing. Name the ranges to be printed. You might put reports on separate sheets, keeping links with the original sheet.

General

Make sure that you follow the specification carefully and give the customers what they want.

Information: Spreadsheet documentation

If a spreadsheet is meant to be kept and reused then it needs to have documentation. This is the paperwork that explains what the spreadsheet is for, how it works and how it should be used. There are two main kinds of documentation. One is **user documentation**. The other is **design documentation**.

User documentation is for the person who will be using the spreadsheet to carry out routine tasks. It gives clear instructions on how to carry out tasks such as opening the spreadsheet, entering new data, saving the data and printing the results. The user may not be an expert spreadsheet user, and need not understand how the spreadsheet was created or how the formulas work.

Design documentation is for the person who needs to understand the spreadsheet. This may be the original designer or it may be someone who comes in later to make alterations to the spreadsheet. Design documentation includes the original specification. It includes all the design sketches, the planned test data and the expected results. It also includes the printouts of the testing and of the final version of the spreadsheet, with descriptions of any modifications.

You are not asked to produce complete or formal documentation at Level 2, but you will be asked to prepare designs and carry out testing.

→ Practise your skills 8.1: Perfect Patios invoice

Perfect Patios now need a spreadsheet that will produce invoices for customers. The invoice should show the company name and address. It should show the customer's name and address, with a phone number in case there are any queries. It should show the date. It should list the names of the items that are bought, the number of items and the unit price. It should calculate the cost for each item. It should work out a subtotal. VAT at 17.5% should then be added to give a subtotal including VAT. Carriage then needs to be added to give the final total. Carriage costs £10 for orders under £500 and £5 for orders of £500 or more.

The company's address is 5 Rivermead Avenue, Southern Trading Estate, Exeter, EX5 9HM.

The invoice should be planned to make data entry easy and give a clear display of results. The people who use the spreadsheet must not be able to damage the spreadsheet by mistake by deleting formulas, etc.

1   Design the spreadsheet on paper. Draw an initial sketch of the layout. Draw a second sketch showing formatting and printing information, including any named ranges to be used. Draw a third sketch showing the formulas you will use. Write notes on your sketches where necessary to explain your decisions.

2   Choose suitable test data. Your spreadsheet will include an IF function so you will need to test with marginal data as well as the other data. Work out the results you would expect using your test data and write them down.

3   Create the spreadsheet according to your design. Save it as **PatioInvoice.xls.**

4   Make any necessary alterations to improve the layout or formatting and write down a note of these changes.

5   Input each of your sets of test data in turn. Print out the results each time and compare them with your expected results. Make any necessary corrections.

6   Save the corrected spreadsheet.

7   Print out the formulas.

8   Close the spreadsheet.

You will learn to

- Use the Office Assistant
- Use the Excel Help menu

Information: Help

Software companies used to include large and comprehensive manuals with their products. This is becoming less common. You may buy software and find that you have little or no documentation on paper that tells you how to use it. Onscreen help is likely to be your main source of reference. It may even include a complete tutorial for you to work through on screen.

Excel has a comprehensive Help facility that includes just about everything you might ever want to know about Excel. The difficult part can be finding the information you want. The Help menu is not always easy for beginners to use because there is just so much there and it takes a while to learn how to use it efficiently.

You are no longer a beginner. As you approach the end of Level 2, you should be using Excel Help more and more. When you are using Excel in the workplace or at home and you want to know how to carry out a task, where will you turn? You should be able to turn to Excel Help. It is best to start by looking up topics that you already know, to get used to the system. You can then move on to look up topics that you do not know.

Task 9.1   Use the Office Assistant

The Office Assistant is provided as a user-friendly way of using the Help facilities. It can come up with the answers you need, but only if you ask your questions using the right words. Some people like using the Office Assistant. Other people hate it and keep it switched off. You want to find out how to use the Help facilities? Why not try asking the Office Assistant about getting help.

Method

I   You may have the Office Assistant displayed on your screen. The Office Assistant can have various forms. It can be a paper clip, a ball, a cat, a dog, a man, a robot and so on. If you can see the Office Assistant, then left click on it to display a yellow box headed 'What would you like to do?'

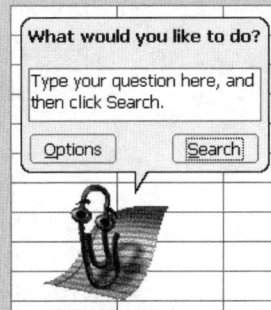

Figure 9.1 The Office Assistant

2 If you cannot see the Office Assistant then click on the Help menu and select 'Show the Office Assistant'. The Office Assistant should appear and you can click on it to show the yellow box as before.

3 The text in the white section of the box should be selected. Key in **Help** to replace this text, then click the button labelled Search.

4 A list of suggestions appears under 'What would you like to do?' The Office Assistant gave me the following list:

- About Microsoft technical resources
- Guidelines for searching Help
- Use Help without the Office Assistant
- About getting help while you work
- Troubleshoot Help
- See more. . .

5 The most promising option seems to be 'About getting help while you work'. Click on this option.

6 A new Help window opens on top of the Excel window. On the right are some headings on your chosen topic. Click the triangle by each heading to show the topics. Read through the information on the screen. You will find out about the various ways of getting help using Microsoft Office.

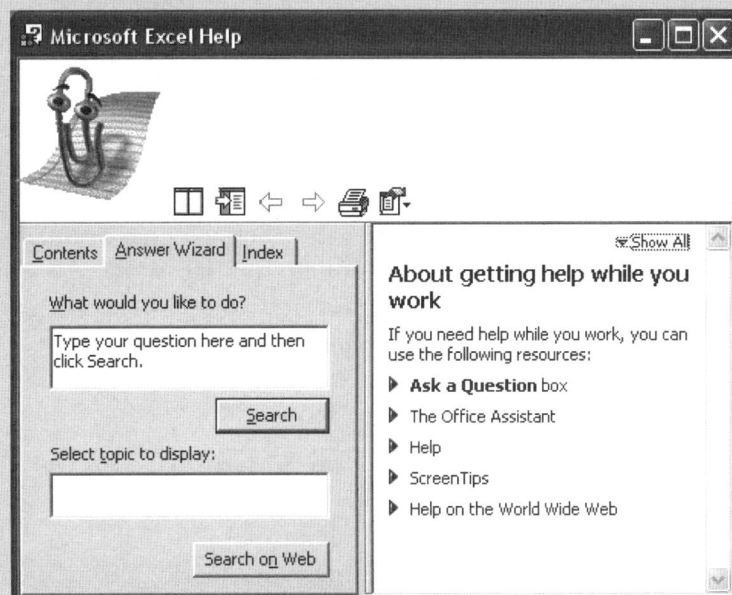

Figure 9.2 The Help window

7 If you find useful information in a Help window then you can print it out. Use the printer icon on the toolbar at the top of the Help window.

8   The toolbar icons from left to right are Autotile, Hide/Show, Back, Forward, Print and Options. Point the mouse at an icon without clicking to see a label with the name of the icon. If you use hyperlinks to navigate between Help pages then the Back icon will take you back to the previous pages you visited. You can then use the Forward icon to move forward again through your visited pages.

9   Click on the Hide (or Show) icon a few times. This swaps between the full Help window and the right hand section only. The right hand section displays the Help topics. The left-hand section gives you access to the whole of the Help facility. There are three tabs labelled Contents, Answer Wizard and Index. You will explore these later.

10   Try out the Autotile icon. This puts your Help window by the side of your spreadsheet instead of on top. The icon changes to the Untile icon which puts the Help window back on top.

11   Close the Help window by clicking on the X button in its top right corner.

Information: Choosing a question to ask the Office Assistant

A single word, Help, produced suggestions that included the information we needed. Often you will need to put in more than one word. Does the way you ask your question affect the answers you get? To find out, click on the Office Assistant and ask your question in different ways. Look at the list of suggestions you get each time. Here are some of my questions and the lists of suggestions they produced. You might like to try other variations.

How can I get help?
- About Microsoft technical resources
- Guidelines for searching Help
- About getting help while you work
- Troubleshoot Help
- See more . . .

Help with Excel
- Use Help without the Office Assistant
- Install or remove individual components in Microsoft Office
- Get help in Microsoft Script Editor
- Learn how to use Microsoft Excel by using Help for Lotus 1-2-3 users
- Troubleshoot online meetings
- See more . . .

Show me how to use the Help menu
- Change the language of the user interface or Help in Office programs
- Things you can do and say with speech recognition
- Show or hide the Ask a Question box
- Show or hide shortcut keys in ScreenTips
- Upgrading from earlier product versions
- See more . . .

→

If you do not find what you want first time, try asking your question in a different way. Include relevant words and leave out words that could be misleading. You can leave out polite padding such as 'Please show me how to' or 'How do I'.

| **Task 9.2** | **Get help using the Contents list, with the Office Assistant switched off** |

Many people like to work with the Office Assistant turned off, and it may be turned off on the system you are using. In this task you will work with the Office Assistant turned off. You will open the Help window and use the Contents list to look for information on relative and absolute references.

Method

1   Turn off the Office Assistant. To do this, right click on the Office Assistant and select Options from the pop-up menu.
2   The Office Assistant dialogue box opens with the Options tab in front. Find the check box labelled 'Use the Office Assistant' and click in it to remove the tick. Click OK. The Office Assistant disappears. (You can get it back using the Help menu if you want it again.)
3   Click on the Help menu and select Microsoft Excel Help. If you see only the right hand part of the Help window then click the Show icon to show both parts.
4   The left part of the window has three tabs: Contents, Answer Wizard and Index. Look at the Contents section.

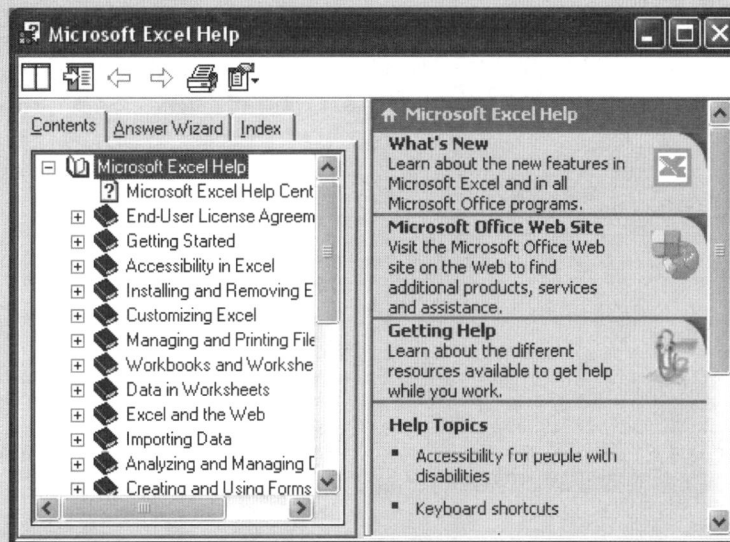

Figure 9.3 The Help window showing the Contents list

5   At first you will probably just see 'Microsoft Excel Help' with a closed book and a + sign. Click on the + sign to open the book.
6   The Contents list is on several levels, with the main sections on the far left and sub-sections indented. A section is shown by a closed book and a plus sign. If you click on the plus sign, the section opens. An open book and a minus sign show that the section is open. You can see the sub-sections and topics within them. The topics themselves are shown with question marks. You click on your chosen topic and it will be displayed in the right hand part of the window.

7   Look down the main list of sections. Where might we find relative and absolute references? The section called 'Creating and correcting formulas' seems possible because references are used in formulas. Click on the plus sign to open the section.

8   Look down the list of sub-sections. 'Creating formulas' seems likely, so click its plus sign to open it. Then open the section called 'Using References'.

9   One of the topics is called 'About cell and range references'. Click on this topic.

10   The Help page appears on the right of the window. One of the topics is 'The difference between relative and absolute references'. Read through the topic and print out the page.

Task 9.3	Get help using the Index

It may be easier to search using the Index. To do this, you choose the keyword which best describes the topic you want. In this task you will look for information on how to print on one page.

Method

1   The Help window should still be open. If not, click on the Help menu and select Microsoft Excel Help.

2   In the left part of the Help window, click on the Index tab.

3   The first box in the Index is labelled 'Type keywords'. Key in **print**.

4   Click the Search button. A list of topics to do with printing appears in the third box. Not surprisingly, there are a lot of topics.

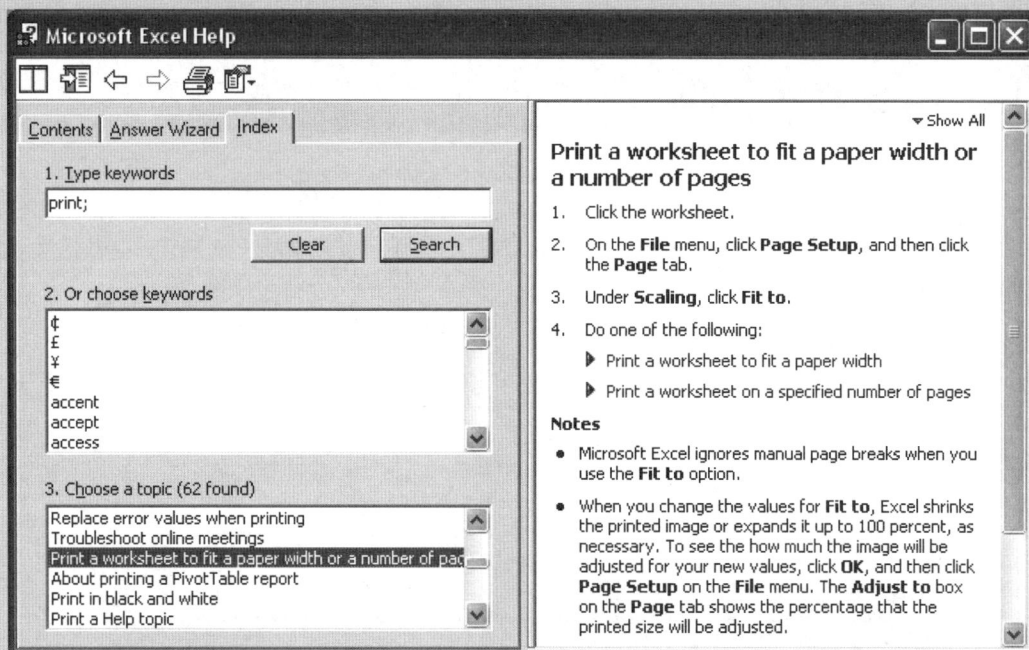

Figure 9.4 The Help window showing the Index

5   One of the topics on the list is 'Print a worksheet to fit a paper width or a number of pages'. You will need to scroll down to find it. Click on this topic and it should show in the right of the window. Read through the topic.

Task 9.4   Get help using the Answer Wizard

The Answer Wizard is like the Office Assistant. It lets you type in your question. You will use it to find information about printing a selected range of cells.

Method

1. Click on the Answer Wizard tab.
2. In the top box, labelled 'What do you want to do?', key in **print selected range of cells**. Click Search.
3. A list of topics appears in the lower box. Click on 'Define what part of the worksheet to print'. The topic appears on the right.
4. Click on the headings and read through the topics.

Task 9.5   Compare ways of getting help

You have learned to get help by using the Office Assistant, the Contents list, the Index and the Answer Wizard. Using these methods you have found information about using the Help facilities, relative and absolute references, printing on one page and printing a selected range of cells.

Try to find the same information but by using different methods. For example, look for information about relative and absolute references by using the Index and by using the Answer Wizard. Which methods do you find easiest to use?

Try to get into the habit of using Excel Help often. The more you use it the easier it will become.

> ### ➔ Practise your skills 9.1: Use Help to investigate unfamiliar topics
>
> Most of the topics you have looked for so far have been familiar topics. You should also try looking up unfamiliar topics using different help methods. Here are some suggested topics. None of them is required for Level 2.
>
> Use Help to find out the answers to the following questions:
>
> 1. What is the keyboard shortcut that will quickly create a chart using the data from selected cells?
> 2. How could you draw shapes such as ovals or squares on a worksheet?
> 3. How could you sort a list of names alphabetically in ascending order?
> 4. How could you find the value of pi? (Pi is a number used in maths for finding the area of a circle, and for other purposes. You cannot find its exact value but Excel can give you a good approximation.)
> 5. Is there an Excel function that can convert miles to kilometres?
> 6. Print out a list of all the shortcut keys that you can use with Excel.
> 7. Is it possible for an Excel workbook to contain a virus?
> 8. What is the ROUNDUP function and how do you use it?
> 9. What is a circular reference?
> 10. What are conditional formats and how can you use them to highlight cells that meet specific conditions?

Using Excel with other MS Office applications

You will learn to

- Paste a screen shot into MS Word and print it out
- Paste data from Excel into a table in MS Word
- Embed an Excel spreadsheet into MS Word
- Paste data from Excel into MS Word, keeping a link
- Paste a chart from Excel into MS Word
- Paste data from a Word table into Excel
- Paste text from Word into Excel
- Import data from a text file

Information: Screen shots

It is possible to capture the image that is displayed on the screen and put it on the clipboard. The image can then be pasted into any kind of file that is able to handle images. It can be printed and it can be saved as part of the file. This method of taking screen shots can provide useful additional evidence to show that you are working correctly. You may be asked to produce screen shots as part of the Level 2 test.

In this section you will learn how to make a screen shot and paste it into a Microsoft Word document. Alternatively, you could paste your screen shots into a document created using Paint, Wordpad, Microsoft Publisher, or even into an Excel workbook.

Before starting the tasks, you need to be able to use Microsoft Word to create a document, key in text, save and print a document.

Hint:

Screen shots are sometimes called screen dumps.

Task 10.1 — Paste a screen shot into MS Word and print it out

You will print out a screen shot showing that you have saved files in your Avondale folder.

Method

1   Start by showing the contents of your Avondale folder on the screen. You can do this by clicking the Start button, selecting My Computer, and then navigating down through the folders until you display the Avondale folder. Alternatively, you can start Excel, click the Open icon on the toolbar and navigate to your Avondale folder in the Open dialogue box.

2   Make sure that the window displaying your Avondale folder is selected. Its name bar should be blue if you use the default Windows colour scheme.

3   Find the Print Screen (or PrnScr) key on your keyboard. This is normally in the top row to the right of the function keys, in a little group of 9 keys. Some keyboards have the key a little lower down, to the right of the backspace delete key. The key may be labelled Print Screen/SysRq.

4   Hold down the Alt key on your keyboard as you press the Print Screen key. Nothing seems to happen, but an image of your selected window is placed on the clipboard.

5   Start up Microsoft Word. A new empty document should be created.

6   Key in **Avondale folder**. Press the Enter key to move to the next line.

7   Give the paste command. You can use the toolbar Paste button or you can select Paste from the Edit menu or you can use the keyboard shortcut Ctrl+v.

8   An image of your Avondale folder should be pasted into your Word document.

9   Save the Word document and print it. You now have hard copy showing the contents of your Avondale folder. You could use this as evidence that you saved the files with the correct names in the correct folder.

Hint:

If you use the Print Screen key by itself, it will capture an image of the whole screen and put it on the clipboard. If you hold down the Alt key as you press Print Screen, it will capture only your selected window.

Information: Integrated applications

Excel is part of the Microsoft Office package, and it is designed to work closely with other applications within Microsoft Office. You will learn how to copy data between Excel and other applications. Copied data can keep a link back to the original data, or it can be independent and have no link. The remainder of this section will be of particular interest to anyone who is planning to take the City & Guilds e-Quals Level 2 Integrated Applications unit. It is not essential for the Spreadsheets Level 2 unit, but the skills introduced here are useful for everyday work. If time is short, you could move on to the practice assignments, then complete this section after taking the real assignment.

Task 10.2   Paste data from Excel into a table in MS Word

You can prepare a report using Word, and paste in a table of data from an Excel workbook.

Method

1   Create a new Word document.

2   Key in a title: **Sales of Cereals**. Key in some text: **Sales of cereals have held up well over the last four years. The table shows our four most popular products.** Press the Enter key twice to leave a clear line.

3   Save the document as **CerealReport**. Leave the document open.

4   Open your Cereals.xls workbook. Select the sheet containing the original data.

5   Select cells A4 to F8, which should contain the data for the sales of cereals.

6   Give the copy command.

7   Switch back to your CerealReport document by clicking on its button on the taskbar at the bottom of the screen.

8   Give the paste command.

9   The data from the selected cells should appear as a Word table. It should look like Table 10.1.

Year	1998	1999	2000	2001	Total
Corn flakes	35	38	40	41	154
Wheat biscuits	27	24	21	22	94
Sugared rice	18	25	24	21	88
Fruit muesli	29	26	20	24	99

Table 10.1 Table pasted in from the Cereals workbook

10   There is no link back to the Excel workbook. There are no formulas in the Word table, so you cannot recalculate. The totals have been pasted in with values only. You can edit the data and manipulate it in Word, just as if the table had been created in Word. If you have learned about Word tables, then you can use your skills to format the table or adapt it to suit your report.

11   Save your Word document.

Task 10.3   Embed an Excel spreadsheet into MS Word

Rather than convert the data from your workbook into a Word table, you might like to keep the formulas available so that you can alter the data and recalculate. You can do this if you embed the workbook in a Word document.

Method

1   Create a new Word document.

2   Key in a title: **Interactive Sales of Cereals**. Key in some text: **Sales of cereals are shown below. Some figures are estimated. You can make changes and recalculate the totals when the final figures are available.** Press the Enter key twice to leave a clear line.

3 Save the document as **CerealEmbedded**. Leave the document open.

4 Switch back to your Cereals.xls workbook. Cells A4 to F8 should still be selected. If not, then select them.

5 Give the copy command.

6 Switch back to your CerealEmbedded document by clicking on its button on the taskbar at the bottom of the screen.

7 This is where the method differs from the method for pasting a table. Click on the Edit menu and select Paste Special from the drop down list. The Paste Special dialogue box should appear. This is different from the Paste Special dialogue box that you saw earlier when you pasted within Excel.

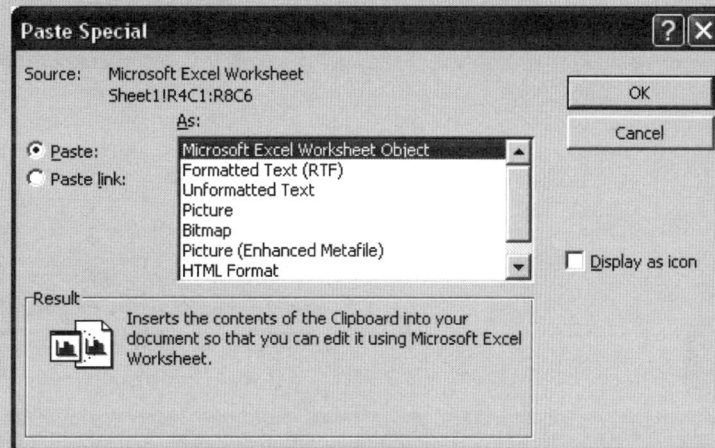

Figure 10.1 Paste Special dialogue box

8 The dialogue box shows that you are pasting data from an Excel worksheet and it gives the cell references. On the left, the Paste option should be selected.

9 Select 'Microsoft Excel Worksheet Object' from the list in the centre of the dialogue box. Below the list you see a message saying that you will insert the contents of the clipboard so that you can edit it using Microsoft Excel Worksheet.

10 Click OK.

11 Your selected cells are inserted as a worksheet object. The object shows resize handles (white squares in the corners and on the sides) when it is selected. Click away from the object to deselect it. Click on the object to select it again. You can resize or move the object just as you resized and moved charts on a worksheet.

12 Save the CerealEmbedded document.

13 Double click on the worksheet object. It should now look like Figure 10.2. You can now alter the data and the totals will recalculate just as they did in the original workbook. Try it out.

	A	B	C	D	E	F
4	Year	1998	1999	2000	2001	Total
5	Corn flakes	35	38	40	41	154
6	Wheat biscuits	27	24	21	22	94
7	Sugared rice	18	25	24	21	88
8	Fruit muesli	29	26	20	24	99

Line graph \ Sheet1 / Sheet2 / Sheet3 /

Figure 10.2 Embedded worksheet object

14 You have a copy of the whole of the original workbook. Try scrolling up or down the sheet and try switching to other sheets. The display is probably not very good, but the content is all there. Scroll back so the display looks like Figure 10.2 again. There is no link back to your original workbook. You have a complete independent copy of it.

15 Click away from the worksheet object to deselect it.

16 Close your CerealEmbedded document, saving any changes.

Task 10.4 — Paste data from Excel into MS Word, keeping a link

Method

1 Create a new Word document.

2 Key in a title: **Linked Sales of Cereals**. Key in some text: **Sales of cereals are shown below. The figures are linked back to the Cereals workbook and will be updated when the workbook changes.** Press the Enter key twice to leave a clear line.

3 Save the document as **CerealLinked**. Leave the document open.

4 Switch back to your Cereals.xls workbook. Cells A4 to F8 should still be selected. If not, then select them.

5 Give the copy command.

6 Switch back to your CerealLinked document by clicking on its button on the taskbar at the bottom of the screen.

7 Click on the Edit menu and select Paste Special from the drop down list. The Paste Special dialogue box should appear just as it did before.

8 On the left of the dialogue box, select the Paste Link option.

9 Select 'Microsoft Excel Worksheet Object' from the list in the centre of the dialogue box as you did before. Below the list you see a message saying that you will insert the contents of the clipboard as a picture. Changes in the original source will be reflected in the copy.

10 Click OK.

11 Your selected cells are inserted. The object shows resize handles when it is selected, and it looks like the embedded worksheet. It behaves differently though. If you double click, the original workbook will open. Any changes you make to the original worksheet will be reflected in the linked object in your Word document. You could try this out.

12 Save the CerealLinked document and close it.

Hint:

When you paste, the little Paste icon appears at the bottom right of the data you have pasted. Point the mouse to the icon and click the arrow that appears. A menu lets you choose Paste options. This is an alternative to using Edit – Paste Special. The icon does not give as many options as Paste Special.

Information: File sizes after pasting, embedding and linking

You have learned three methods of copying data from an Excel workbook to a Word document. Pasting puts the data in a Word table. There is no link to the original workbook. You cannot recalculate, but you can edit the table like any other Word table. Embedding creates a →

copy of the complete workbook and saves it in the Word document. You can edit the workbook and recalculate, but there is no link back to the original. Linking creates a shortcut link back to the original workbook. Any changes in the original workbook will be reflected in the copy.

Your choice of method will depend on how you want to use the data, but there is another consideration, and that is the size of the Word document. The sizes of my three Word documents are as follows:

CerealReport	21 KB
CerealEmbedded	32 KB
CerealLinked	18 KB

Embedding creates a larger file than linking.

Task 10.5 — Paste a chart from Excel into MS Word

Method

1   Your Cereals.xls workbook and your CerealReport document are probably still open. If not, then open them both.
2   There should be a column chart on the same worksheet as the data in your Cereals.xls workbook. Select the chart.
3   Give the copy command.
4   Switch to your CerealReport document by using its button on the taskbar.
5   Leave two clear lines below your table.
6   Click on the Edit menu and select Paste Special. The dialogue box appears.
7   Make sure that the Paste option is selected, and choose 'Microsoft Excel Chart Object' from the list. Click OK.
8   The chart appears in your document. It can be selected and deselected, resized and moved.
9   Double click on the chart. You can edit and format the chart. A Chart menu appears on the menu bar. You can use this, or you can right click on different areas of the chart and use the pop-up menus in the usual way. There is no link back to the original chart.
10 Save and close your CerealReport document. Close your workbook.

Hint:

You can put a chart into a Word document and link it back to the original chart. Use the method of Task 10.5, but select Paste Link from the Paste Special dialogue box.

Hint:

Do you need a break? It might be a good idea to take a break before starting Task 10.6.

Task 10.6 — Paste data from a Word table into Excel

You need to start with a table in Word. You may know how to create a table. If so, you can create your own table in a new Word document. If not, you can do as the Method suggests and use the table that you pasted into your CerealReport document. The fact that the data in the table came originally from Excel makes no difference.

Method

1   Open your CerealReport document.
2   Select the whole of the table. You can do this by 'swiping' the table with the mouse. Alternatively, you can click on the little box that appears outside the top left-hand corner of the table when the mouse points to the table. If these methods are difficult, click anywhere in the table, click on the Table menu and choose Select from the drop down list, then choose Table from the submenu.
3   Give the copy command.
4   Create a new Excel workbook. Select cell A3 (or any other cell of your choice).
5   Give the paste command.
6   The data appears in the spreadsheet cells. You may need to adjust the column widths. There are no formulas. There is no link back to the original table.
7   Save your new workbook with the name **Cereal from Word**.
8   Close your workbook.

Task 10.7   Paste text from Word into Excel

You can select a paragraph of straightforward text in a Word document, copy it, and paste it into a single Excel workbook cell. You could try this on your own. In this task you will paste text that has been put in columns using tabs.

Method

1   Create a new Word document and key in text as follows. Use the tab key to create the columns. Press Enter at the end of each row.
    Special offers on tools
    A163   DIY Cordless drill   £55
    A245   Trade cordless drill   £95
    A174   DIY Angle grinder   £52
    A188   DIY Orbital sander   £55
2   Select the text. Give the copy command.
3   Create a new Excel workbook and select cell B3 or any other cell of your choice.
4   Give the paste command. The text will be pasted in. Each row of text is in a new spreadsheet row, and each tabbed column of text is in a new spreadsheet column. You may need to adjust column widths.

Information: Object linking and embedding

Microsoft Office applications, and many other applications that run in the Windows environment, support object linking and embedding (OLE). This is the technology that allows you to use Copy and Paste or Paste Special to embed or link objects from one application to another. You cannot always integrate copied data fully into the new application as you did with Excel and Word tables. Often the data has to be put in as an object, which you may or may not be able to edit.

To find out more about object linking and embedding, and about integrating applications generally, use the Excel Help. Try entering **object linking and embedding** into the Answer Wizard. Select 'Create a link to another cell, workbook or program' from the list. You could also select 'About linking to another workbook or program'. These help topics describe linking and embedding.

Task 10.8 | Import data from a text file

Excel can import plain text into a single cell, but it can also split up text into separate cells if the text is correctly prepared. In this task you will import lists separated by commas. First you will use Copy and Paste, then you will use a special Excel facility for importing text files.

Method

1 Open Notepad. This should be available from your Start button. Select All Programs. Notepad is normally in the Accessories submenu.
2 A new Notepad window opens. Key in text as follows, taking care to put in the commas correctly.
   Special offers on tools
   A163,DIY Cordless drill,£55
   A245,Trade cordless drill,£95
   A174,DIY Angle grinder,£52
   A188,Orbital sander,£55
3 Check the text. It is basically the same as in Task 10.7 but it uses commas in place of tabs.
4 Save the Notepad file as Tools and the .txt extension should automatically be added. You will need to find this file again, so make sure that you know where it is saved. You could save it in the folder with your spreadsheet files.
5 Select the text and give the copy command. There is no toolbar button, but you can use the Edit menu or the Ctrl+c keyboard shortcut.
6 Create a new Excel workbook. Select cell A3 and give the paste command.
7 Each line of text is placed in a single cell. The lists are not split into separate items.

Hint:

Another way of creating a text file is to key in the text using Word, then save the file as a text file. The drop down list at the bottom of the Save As dialogue box gives you a choice of file types, and you can select Text Only from the list.

8 Select cell A10. This will be the starting point for importing the data again.

9 In Excel, click on the Data menu and select Import External Data from the drop down list. Select Import Data from the submenu.

10 The Select Data Source dialogue box opens. Navigate to your Tools.txt file and select it.

11 Click the Open button. The Text Import Wizard starts.

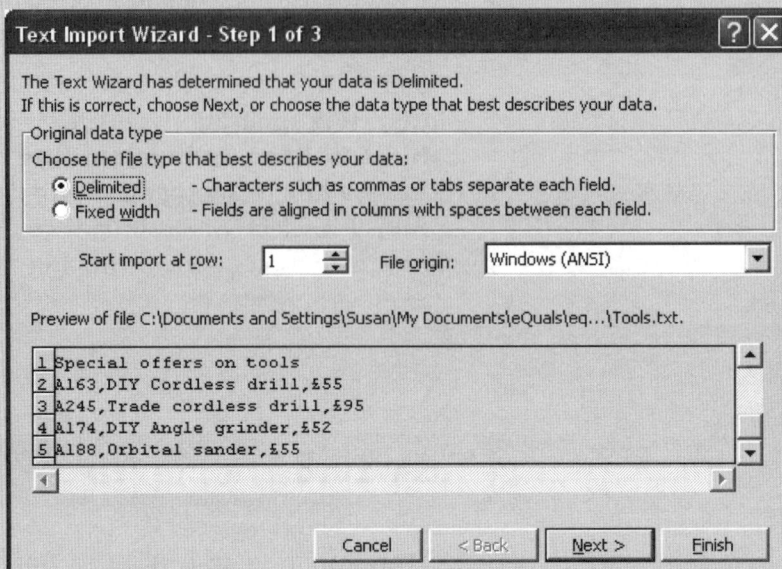

Text Import Wizard - Step 1 of 3　　　　　　　　　　　　　　　　　[?][X]

The Text Wizard has determined that your data is Delimited.
If this is correct, choose Next, or choose the data type that best describes your data.

┌─Original data type───┐
│ Choose the file type that best describes your data: │
│ ⊙ Delimited　　　 - Characters such as commas or tabs separate each field. │
│ ○ Fixed width　　 - Fields are aligned in columns with spaces between each field. │
└──┘

Start import at row:　[1]　⊕　　File origin:　[Windows (ANSI)　▼]

Preview of file C:\Documents and Settings\Susan\My Documents\eQuals\eq...\Tools.txt.

```
1 Special offers on tools
2 A163,DIY Cordless drill,£55
3 A245,Trade cordless drill,£95
4 A174,DIY Angle grinder,£52
5 A188,Orbital sander,£55
```

　　　　　　　　　　[Cancel]　[< Back]　[Next >]　[Finish]

Figure 10.3 Step 1 of the Import Text Wizard

12 The Wizard has detected that the file contains text with items separated by commas or tabs. The File origin box should show Windows (ANSI). Change it if necessary. Click Next.

13 In step 2 of the Wizard, there is a section of the dialogue box that lets you choose the delimiters you want to use. A delimiter is a symbol that separates one item of data from the next. The default is Tab, but one of the alternatives is Comma. Click into the Comma check box to place a tick. You can leave the tick in the Tab box.

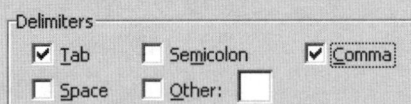

┌─Delimiters────────────────────────────────────┐
│ ☑ Tab　　 ☐ Semicolon　　 ☑ Comma │
│ ☐ Space　 ☐ Other:　[　] │
└───┘

Figure 10.4 Part of step 2 of the Import Text Wizard

14 The lower part of the dialogue box should now show a sample of your text, split up at the comma positions. Click Next.

15 There is no need to change any settings in step 3. Click Finish.

16 A small Import Data dialogue box appears asking where you want to put your data. Keep the default, which should be 'Existing worksheet' and your selected cell A10. Click OK.

17 The text is imported into the workbook, starting at cell A10. The text is split up at the comma positions and goes into separate cells.

18 Save your workbook if you wish, and close it. Close your Notepad file.

Information: Copying between Excel and Access

If you have an existing Access database table, it is possible to select it, copy, and paste the data into an Excel workbook. The data goes into the cells, properly formatted to a suitable data type, and it can be edited normally in Excel.

A range of cells in an Excel worksheet can be copied to an existing Access database table if the range has the same number of columns as the database table, and if these columns have formatting that is compatible with the table. The data from the cells is fully integrated into the database table and can be edited using Access.

There are other ways of transferring data between Excel and Access, but they require a knowledge of Access and will not be described here.

→ Practise your skills 10.1: A report on share prices

You will copy spreadsheet data to a Word table and copy a chart to a Word document.

1 Create a new Word document. Save it as **Share Price Report** and key in the following title and text:

Share Price Report

The price of shares in our three subsidiary companies showed some increase in the period from January 1998 to April 1999. More recent prices have been less encouraging and are available on request.

2 Leave two clear lines below the text.

3 Open your Shares.xls workbook.

4 Copy the share prices from cells A1 to D8 and paste them into your Word document.

5 Leave two clear lines below the table of share prices.

6 Your workbook should contain a line graph showing the share prices of the three companies. Copy this chart and paste it into your Word document.

7 Resize the chart if necessary.

8 Key in your name after the chart.

9 Save the Word document, print it and close it.

10 Close your Shares.xls workbook.

Practice assignments

In order to achieve the Level 2 spreadsheet qualification, you need to take and pass one assignment. There are Pass, Credit and Distinction grades available. Your tutor will give you the real assignment when you and your tutor agree that you are ready.

You will be producing written and printed work. Your tutor will also need to check your saved files. Your tutor will tell you where you should save your files. This may be in a special network area or it may be on a floppy disk. The time allowed may be 4 hours or 6 hours, depending on which test you are given.

You will need a prepared spreadsheet called DAILY for Practice assignment 1. You will need a prepared spreadsheet called WHOLESALE for Practice assignment 2. Your tutor may be able to provide these spreadsheets. If you need to create these spreadsheets yourself, you can find details at the end of this section. Create the DAILY and WHOLESALE spreadsheets before starting the assignments. The time you take creating these spreadsheets is not counted as part of the assignment time.

Practice assignment 1: Grand Hotel

Read all the instructions carefully before starting work.

You must, at all times, observe all relevant health and safety precautions.

Time allowed 4 hours

Introduction

This assignment is in three parts.
Part A requires you to design a spreadsheet data entry form.
Part B requires you to create and test the data entry form.
Part C requires you to extract data from an existing spreadsheet into a new spreadsheet, perform calculations and prepare charts.

> **Scenario**
>
> The Grand Hotel management has decided to update their computer system. Reception staff will be able to check guests in by keying in the details directly to the system. You are asked to design and produce a spreadsheet data entry form.
>
> The data entry form should display the hotel name and the title 'Check in'. It should show the current date. There should be space to enter the guest's name, address and phone number, the room number, the room type (standard or luxury), and the number of nights the guest plans to stay. The cost of the room per night should be displayed automatically, depending on the room type. Standard rooms are £50 and luxury rooms are £60. The total cost for the stay should be calculated.

Your data entry form should include prompts to help the user enter the correct data. If the postcode has not been entered, a message should be displayed to say that the postcode must be entered. Room numbers are from 100 to 500. If the user enters a room number less than 100 or greater than 500 then an appropriate message should be displayed. You could use two separate formulas to display the messages, or you could combine them into one formula. The user should be prompted to enter S for a standard room or L for a luxury room. The prompt should be displayed when there is no entry for the room type. If there is no entry or an incorrect entry for room type then the price for the luxury room may be displayed.

Task A

1 Produce a design on paper to include
- the structure and layout of the spreadsheet, including data labels, titles and data input areas
- the formatting, including alignment, font and font size, enhancements (bold, etc.), number type (date, currency, decimal places), borders, shading, hidden or protected cells
- definition of any printouts required, including page size, orientation, headers and footers
- definition of formulas and functions to be used.

Label your design sheets DESIGN1, DESIGN2, etc.

2 Choose test data that will test all formulas. There should be at least five sets of test data.

3 Calculate the expected results from the test data. Label your sheet(s) EXPECTED RESULTS.

Task B

1 Access the spreadsheet application, create a new spreadsheet and save it with the name CHECKIN in a new directory called HOTEL.

2 Create the data entry form according to your design. Improve and adjust the design as necessary.

3 Print a copy of the spreadsheet on one sheet of paper to show the formulas. Include gridlines, column letters and row numbers. Label this printout CHECKIN1. Write notes on the printout if necessary to describe any changes you have made to the design.

4 Test your spreadsheet using your test data. Make any necessary corrections. Produce a printout to show the results from each set of test data. Label your printouts TEST1, TEST2, etc. If you have made corrections to formulas then write a note on one of the printouts to say what corrections you have made.

Task C

The hotel keeps a daily record of the number of rooms occupied and the takings from the bar and restaurant. You will be asked to extract data from this record and use it to produce a report, illustrated by charts, of the income for one week.

1 Copy the prepared spreadsheet called DAILY into your HOTEL directory. Open the spreadsheet.

2 Copy the column headings and the figures for the first 7 days of September and paste them into a new spreadsheet without making any links. Save the new spreadsheet with the name SEPTWEEK1 into your HOTEL directory.

3 Insert two columns between Standard rooms occupied and Bar takings. Give these columns the headings Luxury rooms and Standard rooms. Your SEPTWEEK1 spreadsheet should now have column headings as shown.

	A	B	C	D	E	F	G
3	**Date**	**Luxury rooms occupied**	**Standard rooms occupied**	**Luxury rooms**	**Standard rooms**	**Bar takings**	**Restaurant**
4	01/09/02	31	28			£ 157	£ 495

Table 11.1 Column headings for SEPTWEEK1

4 Leave at least two clear rows below the main part of the spreadsheet. In unoccupied cells below this, enter the cost per night for a standard room (£50) and for a luxury room (£60). Add suitable descriptive labels.

5 In the Luxury rooms column, enter a formula to find the income from letting luxury rooms on 01/09/02. Replicate this formula to find the income for 02/09/02, 03/09/02 and so on.

6 In the Standard rooms column, enter a formula to find the income from letting standard rooms on 01/09/02. Replicate this formula to find the income for 02/09/02, 03/09/02 and so on.

7 In the row below the entries for 07/09/02, enter formulas to find the total income for the week from luxury rooms, standard rooms, bar and restaurant.

8 Add a title for the sheet and add any appropriate formatting.

9 Create a pie chart to show what percentage of the total income came from luxury rooms, standard rooms, bar and restaurant. Include suitable titles and labels. Place the chart on the sheet with the data. Move and resize it as necessary to give a good printed display.

10 Print the spreadsheet showing the results and the pie chart. Label the printout REPORT1.

11 Print the formulas showing gridlines, column letters and row numbers on one sheet of paper. Do not include any charts in the printout. Label the printout REPORT2.

12 Create a line graph to show how the income from each of the sources has varied from day to day over the week. Include suitable titles and labels or legend. Lines should be clearly distinguishable when printed.

13 Print the line graph on its own sheet of paper. Label the printout REPORT3.

14 Save and close all spreadsheets and close the spreadsheet application.

Note
- At the conclusion of this assignment, hand all paperwork and disks to the test supervisor.
- Ensure that your name is on the disk (if using a floppy disk) and all documentation.
- If the assignment is taken over more than one period, all floppy disks and paperwork must be returned to the test supervisor at the end of each sitting.

Practice assignment 2: Home Maker

Read all the instructions carefully before starting work.

You must, at all times, observe all relevant health and safety precautions.

Time allowed 4 hours

Introduction

This assignment is in three parts.
Part A requires you to design a spreadsheet data entry form.
Part B requires you to create and test the data entry form.
Part C requires you to import data from an existing spreadsheet, keeping a link, and perform calculations.

> **Scenario**
>
> The Home Maker company has a store selling a wide range of items for the home. They have recently produced a catalogue so that customers can order by post or phone. You are asked to produce a data entry form to be used by sales staff when customers place an order by phone. The staff member should be able to key in details of the order as the customer speaks, confirm the details, and tell the customer the total cost of the order, including postage and packing. The form can then be printed.
>
> The form should show:
> The company name, the order number and the current date
> The customer's name, address and phone number
> The catalogue number, name and unit price of up to six items
> The number of each item ordered.
>
> Calculate the total cost for each item. Show the cost of all the items as a subtotal. If the subtotal is less than £10 then postage and packing is charged at 10% of the subtotal amount, otherwise it is charged at 5% of the subtotal amount. Calculate the grand total.

Task A

1 Produce a design on paper to include
   - the structure and layout of the spreadsheet, including data labels, titles and data input areas
   - the formatting, including alignment, font and font size, enhancements (bold, etc.), number type (date, currency, decimal places), borders, shading, hidden or protected cells
   - definition of any printouts required, including page size, orientation, headers and footers
   - definition of formulas and functions to be used.

   Label your design sheets DESIGN1, DESIGN2, etc.

2 Choose test data that will test all formulas. There should be at least five sets of test data.

3 Calculate the expected results from the test data. Label your sheet(s) EXPECTED RESULTS.

Task B

1. Access the spreadsheet application, create a new spreadsheet and save it with the name ORDER in a new directory called HOMEMAKER.

2. Create the data entry form according to your design. Improve and adjust the design as necessary.

3. Print a copy of the spreadsheet on one sheet of paper to show the formulas. Include gridlines, column letters and row numbers. Label this printout ORDER1. Write notes on the printout if necessary to describe any changes you have made to the design.

4. Test your spreadsheet using your test data. Make any necessary corrections. Produce a printout to show the results from each set of test data. Label your printouts TEST1, TEST2, etc. If you have made corrections to formulas then write a note on one of the printouts to say what corrections you have made.

Task C

1. Copy the prepared spreadsheet called WHOLESALE into your HOMEMAKER directory. Open the WHOLESALE spreadsheet. This shows items that Home Maker can buy as a special purchase to include in their seasonal sales. Each item has a category: T for textile or N for non-textile. The wholesaler quotes a unit price and a minimum order number.

2. Copy the table of data from cells A3 to D19 of the WHOLESALE spreadsheet. Paste the table of data to a new spreadsheet, starting at cell A3 and keeping a link with the original data. Save the new spreadsheet with the name SALE into your HOMEMAKER directory.

3. Enter a title 'Summer Sale Special Purchase' in cell A1.

4. Enter additional column headings as shown.

	E	F	G	H	I	J
3	Cost to buy	Markup	Selling price	No sold	Takings	Profit

Table 11.2 Additional column headings for SALE worksheet

5. Home Maker buys the minimum number of each item. Enter a formula to find the cost to buy the minimum number of the first item. Replicate this formula for the remaining items.

6. Home Maker adds a markup of 70% of their unit purchase price for textile items and a markup of 120% of their unit purchase price for non-textile items. Enter a formula to work out the markup for the first item. The formula should automatically give the right markup, depending on whether the item is textile or non-textile. Replicate this formula for the remaining items.

7. Add the markup to the unit price to find the selling price for the first item. Use a function to round the value to 2 decimal places. Formatting to 2 decimal places is not sufficient, as further calculations must use the rounded value. Replicate this formula for the remaining items.

8. Leave the No sold column empty for the moment.

9. Enter a formula to work out the takings for the first item. If the entry for No sold is greater than the number of items bought, then there should be a message displaying 'error' instead of the value for the takings. Replicate this formula for the remaining items.

10 Enter a formula to find the profit for the first item. Replicate this formula for the remaining items.

11 Enter formulas to find the totals of the Cost to buy, Takings and Profit columns.

12 Format the spreadsheet appropriately, and protect it so that only the data input cells can be edited. Add your name, the date and the file name in a header and/or footer.

13 Test the spreadsheet by entering test values in the No sold column. Print a copy of the spreadsheet showing that the error message is displayed where appropriate. The printout should be on one sheet of paper. Label the printout SALE1.

14 Enter the number of each item sold in the summer sale. The values are given in the following table.

Item	No sold Summer	No sold Autumn
Pack of 4 cushion covers	15	20
Throw 125 × 150 cm	10	8
Throw 200 × 250 cm	10	4
Chequer design rug	12	13
Runner mat	10	18
Flower pattern seat pad	6	12
24 piece cutlery set	20	20
20 piece gold band dinnerware	8	10
Brown baking dish	20	14
20 piece blue pattern dinnerware	7	8
Plain dye bath towel	42	56
Patterned bath towel	38	46
Bath mat set	32	25
Duvet set	20	15
Electric steamer	10	7
Kettle	8	10

Table 11.3 Numbers of items sold

15 Print the spreadsheet on one sheet of paper. Label the printout SALE2.

16 Home Maker buy items for their autumn sale. Again they buy the minimum number of each item on the list. There are some changes to the list. Make the following alterations to the original WHOLESALE spreadsheet.

Pack of 4 cushion covers, new price £6.10
Chequer design rug, new price £3.75
Plain dye bath towel, new price £0.80, new minimum order 60

17 Save the WHOLESALE spreadsheet.

18 In the SALE spreadsheet, change the title to show Autumn Sale instead of Summer Sale.

19 Replace the No sold values with the Autumn values from Table 11.3.

20 Save the SALE spreadsheet.

21 Print the spreadsheet on one sheet of paper. Label the printout SALE3.

22 Print the formulas on not more than two sheets of paper showing gridlines, row numbers and column letters. Label the printouts SALE4.

23 Close all spreadsheets and close the spreadsheet application.

Note

- At the conclusion of this assignment, hand all paperwork and disks to the test supervisor.
- Ensure that your name is on the disk (if using a floppy disk) and all documentation.
- If the assignment is taken over more than one period, all floppy disks and paperwork must be returned to the test supervisor at the end of each sitting.

DAILY spreadsheet for Practice assignment 1

	A	B	C	D	E
1	**Grand Hotel daily record**				
2					
3	Date	Luxury rooms occupied	Standard rooms occupied	Bar takings	Restaurant
4	01/09/02	31	28	£ 157	£ 495
5	02/09/02	50	52	£ 207	£ 921
6	03/09/02	47	60	£ 248	£ 1,183
7	04/09/02	53	59	£ 294	£ 1,038
8	05/09/02	44	49	£ 201	£ 991
9	06/09/02	32	46	£ 182	£ 853
10	07/09/02	20	13	£ 156	£ 520
11	08/09/02	34	27	£ 209	£ 739
12	09/09/02	56	45	£ 268	£ 1,288
13	10/09/02	51	53	£ 241	£ 1,190

Table 11.4 DAILY spreadsheet

WHOLESALE spreadsheet for Practice assignment 2

	A	B	C	D
1	**Price to buy from wholesaler**			
2				
3	Category	Item	Unit price	Minimum order
4	T	Pack of 4 cushion covers	£ 6.00	20
5	T	Throw 125 × 150 cm	£ 3.00	10
6	T	Throw 200 × 250 cm	£ 6.00	10
7	T	Chequer design rug	£ 3.50	15
8	T	Runner mat	£ 6.25	20
9	T	Flower pattern seat pad	£ 0.50	20
10	T	24 piece cutlery set	£ 5.50	20
11	N	20 piece gold band dinnerware	£ 12.00	10
12	N	Brown baking dish	£ 0.50	20
13	N	20 piece blue pattern dinnerware	£ 13.50	10
14	T	Plain dye bath towel	£ 0.75	50
15	T	Patterned bath towel	£ 1.05	50
16	T	Bath mat set	£ 4.00	50
17	T	Duvet set	£ 5.00	20
18	N	Electric steamer	£ 15.00	10
19	N	Kettle	£ 14.50	10

Table 11.5 WHOLESALE spreadsheet

Solutions

Section 1 Spreadsheet basics
Check your knowledge

1 Text (labels), numbers (values) and formulas.

2 You can change the numbers and the formulas will recalculate the results.

3 .xls

4 A, B, E, F

5 Editing

6 Formatting

7 A range is a collection of two or more cells. It is often a rectangular block of cells, but in modern versions of Excel it does not have to be rectangular.

8 C7, C8, C9, D7, D8, D9, E7, E8, E9.

9 The cells are displayed as twice their original width. The width is halved again when you return to the normal view showing results.

10 When you change to formula view, it may be necessary to change column widths in order to display formulas in full. Beginners are normally told not to change column widths in formula view. When you are more advanced and start using very long formulas, you cannot avoid changing widths. You may also want to make some columns narrower to fit the spreadsheet on the page. These changes should not be saved because they will alter the display in normal view. You therefore save the widths you want in normal view and do not save again with the altered widths.

Section 2 Spreadsheet layout and formatting
Practise your skills 2.1

Figure 12.1 A Food Survey solution

Practise your skills 2.2

Figure 12.2 An Avondale Hospital solution

Check your knowledge

1 B4 to B7, C4 to C7, H4 to H7. Possibly A4 to A7 too.

2 A1, A3 to J3, E9. Possibly A4 to A7.

3 D4 to G7, I4 to J7, F9 to J9.

4 J4 to J7, F9 to J9. Maybe others. It depends on the use to be made of the spreadsheet.

5 yes

6 yes

7 no

8 yes

9 locked

10 unprotected

11 37512

12 18:00 or 6:00 PM

Section 3 Editing, copying and further display methods
Practise your skills 3.1

	A	B	C	D	E	F	J
1	**Salads**			Date	12/09/02		
2							
3	**Item**	**Supplier**	**No in crate**	**No of crates**	**Price of crate**	**Cost to buy**	**Takings**
4	Lettuces – cos	MacArthur Growers	12	6	£ 5.50	£ 33.00	£ 55.25
5	Lettuces – round	MacArthur Growers	12	6	£ 5.00	£ 30.00	£ 25.62
6	Lettuces – iceberg	MacArthur Growers	8	8	£ 6.00	£ 48.00	£ 63.36
20	Peppers – green	Southern Produce	20	3	£ 2.00	£ 6.00	£ 9.60
21	Peppers – red	Southern Produce	20	3	£ 2.20	£ 6.60	£ 9.02
22	Peppers – yellow	Southern Produce	20	2	£ 2.20	£ 4.40	£ 8.80
40	Tomato – standard	Guernsey Tomatoes	100	3	£ 8.00	£ 24.00	£ 42.15
41	Tomato – cherry	Guernsey Tomatoes	200	2	£ 16.00	£ 32.00	£ 23.60
42	Tomato – beef	Guernsey Tomatoes	50	3	£ 10.00	£ 30.00	£ 34.50
43							
44					Totals	£ 214.00	£ 271.90
45							
46					Gross profit	£ 57.90	
47					Overheads and expenses	£ 25.00	
48					Net profit	£ 32.90	

Figure 12.3 Final printout of Salads spreadsheet

Check your knowledge

1 32

2 35

3 Thursday

4 Alison

5 A large white cross

6 A white arrow pointing to black crossed arrows

7 A small black cross

8 Ctrl (Control)

9 Splitting the window gives two or four separate areas that can each scroll independently. Freezing panes fixes the upper and/or left part of the window and allows the lower and/or right part of the window to scroll.

10 Split the window so that you can scroll one part to show K42 and another part to show Z97.

Section 4 Formulas and functions
Practise your skills 4.1

	A	B	C	D	E
1	**Exports**				=TODAY()
2					
3	Millions of pounds				
4					
5	**Country**	**Year 1**	**Year 2**	**Year 3**	**Year 4**
6	**USA**	12.4	14.3	13.7	16.2
7	**Canada**	9.7	10.5	9.4	
8	**Germany**	15.1	15.8	16.1	16.9
9	**France**	6.2	7.8	12.3	10.5
10					
11	**Total for year**	=SUM(Year1)	=SUM(Year2)	=SUM(Year3)	=SUM(Year4)
12	**Average for year**	=AVERAGE(Year1)	=AVERAGE(Year2)	=AVERAGE(Year3)	=AVERAGE(Year4)
13	**Maximum**	=MAX(Year1)	=MAX(Year2)	=MAX(Year3)	=MAX(Year4)
14	**Minimum**	=MIN(Year1)	=MIN(Year2)	=MIN(Year3)	=MIN(Year4)
15					
16		=COUNT(Year1)	=COUNT(Year2)	=COUNT(Year3)	=COUNT(Year4)
17					
18		=IF(B16=4,"OK","check")	=IF(C16=4,"OK","check")	=IF(D16=4,"OK","check")	=IF(E16=4,"OK","check")

Figure 12.4 Formula printout of Exports2 spreadsheet

The formula in B18 is **=IF(B16=4,"OK","check")**.

Cells B18, C18 and D18 should display **OK**. Cell E18 should display **check** when cell E7 is empty.

Practise your skills 4.2

The new formulas should be as follows:

Cell D3   =IF(B3="","Enter your own name","")
Cell D4   =IF(B4="","Enter your own ID","")
Cell A19 =IF(B14+E15>=35,"Good diet","Consider eating more fruit and veg")

Tests of the IF() functions should include:
Make cell B3 blank and then enter text into it.
Make cell B4 blank and then enter text into it.
Enter numbers so that the total of fruit and vegetable portions comes to 35, 34, 36, a smaller number and a larger number.
You may also have tested with extreme data and rogue data.

Practise your skills 4.3

Formulas in the original version are:

Cell B10 =MAX(B8:D8)
Cell B12 =IF(B8=$B$10,"Winner","")
Cell C12 =IF(C8=$B$10,"Winner","")
Cell D12 =IF(D8=$B$10,"Winner","")

After giving cell B10 a name, the altered formulas are:

Cell B12 =IF(B8=Highest,"Winner","")
Cell C12 =IF(C8=Highest,"Winner","")
Cell D12 =IF(D8=Highest,"Winner","")

Notice that there are no quotes round Highest. It is a cell name, not text in a cell.
If two or three teams tie for first place then both or all will have Winner displayed.

Check your knowledge

1 Today(). Alternatively you could use Now() and format the result to date.

2 132.67

3 Formatting displays the value with the given number of decimal places, but the original number is still stored and used in calculations. The ROUND() function does not keep the original number. It discards the extra decimal places. The rounded number will be used in calculations. =B3*100 would give 13267.18 but =B4*100 would give 13267.00.

4 =$B$1*E3
$B$1 is an absolute reference and does not change. D3 is a relative reference and it changes to E3 when the formula is copied from D4 to E4.

5 =E3*VATrate

6 E3 and B2. VATrate always refers to cell B2 even when a formula is copied.

7 Named cells or ranges can make formulas easier to understand. They can also be used instead of absolute references because the name always refers to the same cell or range of cells.

8 All right

9 Too big

10 Marginal data values: you should use 80 and a number just smaller than 80. 79.99 might be a good choice since you are dealing with money values and pence are likely to be involved. These numbers cover the point where the result of the formula changes. It is usual to include 80.01 as well.

Representative data values: these can be any likely values such as 50 or 100. Choose representative values above and below 80.

Extreme values: use the largest and smallest acceptable values. You could use 0, 1000000, negative numbers if these are allowed.

Rogue values: enter something that is not acceptable.

Consolidation 1

The formula in cell G17 is
=C17*$A$5+D17*$A$6+E17*$A$7+F17*$A$8.
If you have chosen to use named cells then
your names will be in the formula instead of
the absolute references.

The formula in cell B25 is =COUNT(B17:B22).
The COUNT function will not count text cells
so you cannot count the batch references, but
you can count the dates. Alternatively, you
could count the batch references using the
COUNTA function.

The formula in cell A26 is =IF(G23<50,"Extra
articles needed next month","").

The lower part of the Carruthers spreadsheet
should look like Figure 12.5.

15			Number of articles of each type in batch				
16	Batch ref.	Date	Type A	Type B	Type C	Type D	Pay for batch
17	99A001	04/01/02	25	4	0	0	£ 13.20
18	99A002	11/01/02	20	10	1	0	£ 16.90
19	99A003	18/01/02	18	15	0	2	£ 21.60
20	99A004	25/01/02	22	8	0	0	£ 15.20
21							£ -
22							£ -
23		Totals	85	37	1	2	£ 66.90
24							
25		4	batches processed this month.				
26							

Figure 12.5 Part of the Carruthers spreadsheet

The Jackson spreadsheet should display the message in
cell A26. The total pay should be £47.60.

Section 5 Charts and graphs
Practise your skills 5.1

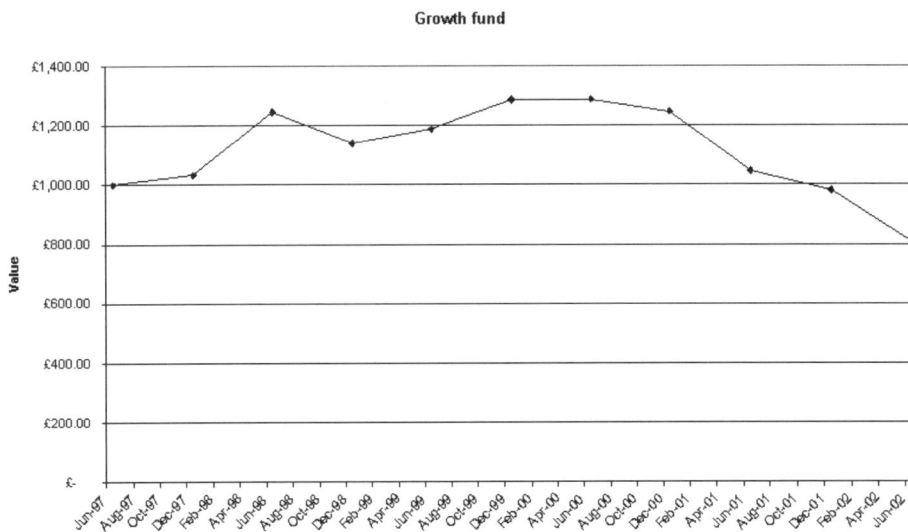

Figure 12.6 Line graph of growth fund

Your formatting may differ from that
shown in Figure 12.7.

A line graph is suitable for displaying the
unit trust data because it shows how the
values change with time.

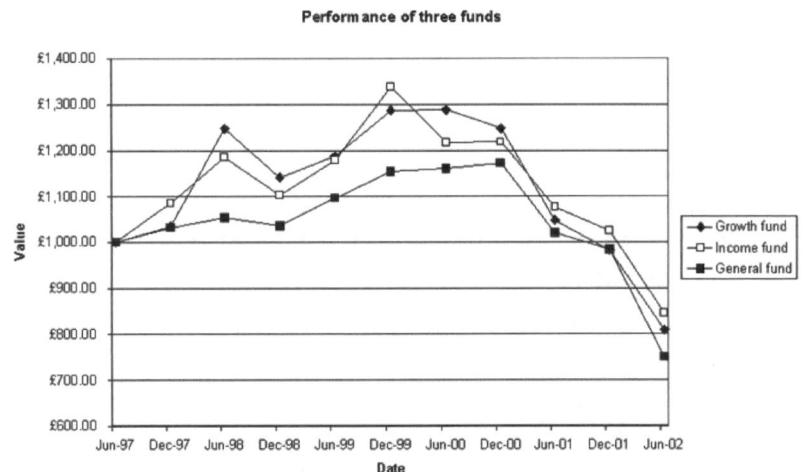

Figure 12.7 Line graph of three funds

Practise your skills 5.2

Sales of Cereals
In metric tonnes

Year	1998	1999	2000	2001	Total
Corn flakes	35	38	40	41	154
Wheat biscuits	27	24	21	22	94
Sugared rice	18	25	24	21	88
Fruit muesli	29	26	20	24	99

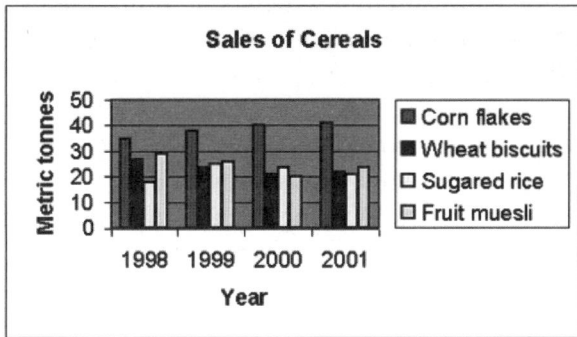

Figure 12.8 Cereals column chart on worksheet

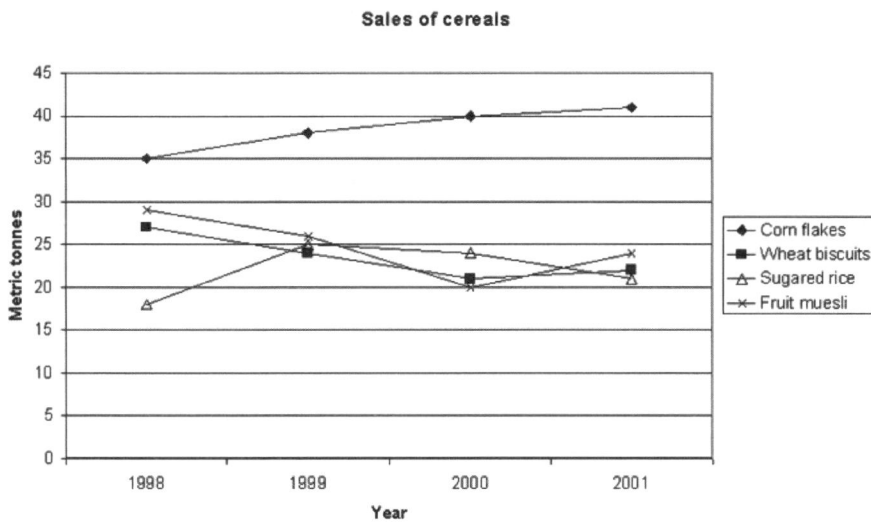

Figure 12.9 Cereals line graph

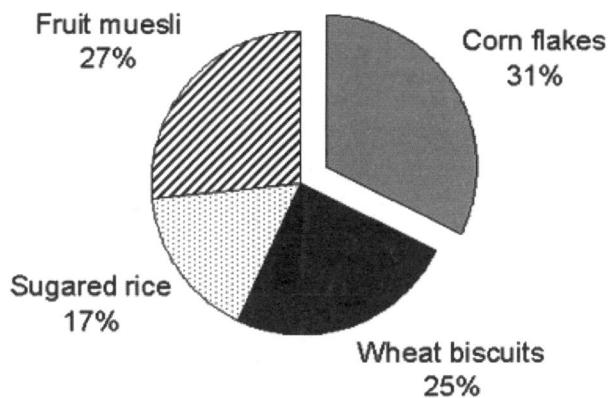

Figure 12.10 Cereals pie chart

Check your knowledge

1 Line – the best choice. It shows trends over equal time intervals.
Column – a possible alternative.
Bar – less good. It puts more emphasis on size rather than time intervals.
Pie – not suitable. It is meaningless to show temperature for one day as % of total.
XY – not suitable. There is no relationship between day number and temperature.

2 Pie – a good choice. It shows numbers as % of the whole.
Bar – also possible. It shows numbers rather than percentages.
Column – also possible.
Line – not suitable. There is no time scale.
XY – not suitable. There are no numbers on the X axis.

3 XY – the best choice for the purpose. It should bring out any relationship between income and the amount people smoke.
Line graph – not really suitable. There is no time scale.
Bar or column – not suitable for the data as it is. There would need to be a lot of bars or columns, one for each person's income, unless the data was grouped into income bands.
Pie chart – not suitable for the data as it is. It could be used if you group the income into bands and want to know what percentage of the total cigarettes are smoked by each income band.

4 Bar or column – most suitable if you want to emphasise the numbers of people using each form of transport.
Pie – most suitable if you want to emphasise the percentages of people using each form of transport.
Line – not suitable. There is no time scale.
XY – not suitable. There are no numbers on the X axis.

5 Excel will plot the empty rows as if they contained zero values.

6 The easiest solution is to key in the year numbers again starting with a single quote to make Excel treat them as text. You can then create the chart again. An alternative is to use step 2 of the Wizard to specify which cells are to be used as labels and which cells are to be used for plotting on the chart.

7 A pie chart with one or more slices pulled outwards to emphasise them.

8 You can't return to the Wizard itself, but all four of its steps are available from the Chart menu. You can use these to continue preparing the chart.

9 Probably the chart is selected. Click out of the chart to deselect it and preview again.

10 Yes. Select the chart. Click on the Chart menu and select Location. You can then choose to put the chart on its own sheet.

Section 6 Using copy and link to import and extract data
Practise your skills 6.1

Swim-fit Swimming Club
Income

	Quarter1	Quarter2	Quarter3	Quarter4
Joining fees	795	710	320	480
Session fees	260	620	1650	560
Donations	54	25	0	60
Sales	640	570	800	520
Other	100	10	25	75

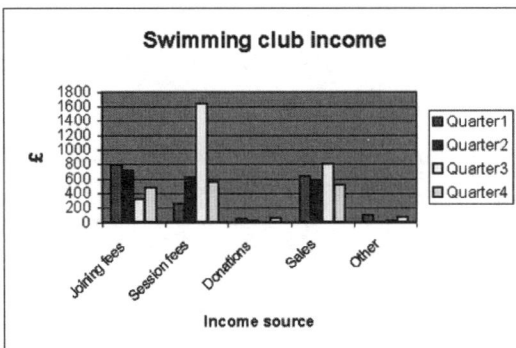

Figure 12.11 The IncomeChart sheet of the SwimQuarterly workbook

Check your knowledge

1 It contains =C1+C2. It displays 5.
2 It still displays 5.
3 It displays 7.
4 D3 contains 5 and it displays 5.
5 It still displays 5. There is no formula so it does not update.
6 Cell E3 contains =A3. It is linked to cell A3. It displays 5.
7 Cell E3 displays 9.
8 Hold down the Ctrl key as you drag.

Consolidation 2

Printout 1 of the summary sheet before changing the rates of pay.

Environmental Science Information Service
Keywords and abstracting by freelance workers

January	Type A	Type B	Type C	Type D	Pay for batch
Carruthers	85	37	1	2	£ 66.90
Jackson	79	20	0	0	£ 47.60
Total	**164**	**57**	**1**	**2**	**£ 114.50**

February	Type A	Type B	Type C	Type D	Pay for batch
Carruthers	88	41	1	2	£ 71.30
Jackson	106	35	6	1	£ 77.00
Total	**194**	**76**	**7**	**3**	**£ 148.30**

March	Type A	Type B	Type C	Type D	Pay for batch
Carruthers	89	47	2	3	£ 78.60
Jackson	93	46	4	2	£ 80.00
Total	**182**	**93**	**6**	**5**	**£ 158.60**

3 Month Total	540	226	14	10	£ 421.40

Figure 12.12 Environmental Science summary sheet

After changing the rates of pay, the 3 Month Total pay is £433.70.

Section 8 Spreadsheet design and testing

Practise your skills 8.1

You should have hand-drawn sketches showing the overall layout, the formatting and the formulas. You should have test data and expected results. The test data should include the marginal values for the IF() function. These are £500 and £499.99. You should also include £500.01. The prices and numbers need to be adjusted so that these marginal values appear as the subtotal including VAT.

You should have printouts showing the testing, and also a printout of formulas. The figure shows one of the printouts produced during testing. Your layout and formatting may be different.

Invoice
Perfect Patios
5 Rivermead Avenue, Southern Trading Estate, Exeter, EX5 9HM

Customer name	A Customer	20/08/02
Customer address	11 Station Road	
	Exmouth	
	Devon	
	EX13 5FF	
Phone number	01234 567890	

Item	No ordered	Unit price	Price
Hamilton paving 300x300	50	£ 1.50	£ 75.00
Hamilton paving 600x300	20	£ 2.00	£ 40.00
Hamilton paving 600x600	100	£ 3.00	£ 300.00
Ornament	1	£ 10.52	£ 10.52
			£ -
			£ -
		Subtotal	£ 425.52
VAT rate	17.50%	VAT	£ 74.47
		Subtotal + VAT	£ 499.99
Carriage £10 if under £500		Carriage	£ 10.00
otherwise £5		Grand total	£ 509.99

Figure 12.13 Perfect Patios invoice spreadsheet

Practice assignments

Practice assignment 1: Grand Hotel

You should have several hand-drawn designs of the data entry form, including all the information specified in Task A.

You should have five handwritten sheets showing your sets of test data and the results of your own calculations.

Your formula printout might look like Figure 12.14.

Grand Hotel

Check in	=TODAY()
Guest name	
Guest address	
Post code	=IF(C10="","Post code must be entered","")
Guest phone	
Room number	=IF(C13<100,"Number must be 100 or higher","")
	=IF(C13>500,"Number must be 500 or lower","")
Room Type	=IF(C15="","Enter S for standard, L for luxury","")
Cost per night	=IF(C15="S",50,60)
Length of stay	
Cost of room	=C16*C17

Figure 12.14 Formula view of the Grand Hotel form

There should be a printout for each set of test data. Data should be chosen to show each message at least once. Both types of room should be used. You should include marginal values for the room numbers.

The spreadsheet part of Report 1 might look like Figure 12 .15. There should also be a pie chart.

Grand Hotel — Income for week starting 01/09/02

Date	Luxury rooms occupied	Standard rooms occupied	Luxury rooms	Standard rooms	Bar takings	Restaurant
01/09/02	31	28	£ 1,860	£ 1,400	£ 157	£ 495
02/09/02	50	52	£ 3,000	£ 2,600	£ 207	£ 921
03/09/02	47	60	£ 2,820	£ 3,000	£ 248	£ 1,183
04/09/02	53	59	£ 3,180	£ 2,950	£ 294	£ 1,038
05/09/02	44	49	£ 2,640	£ 2,450	£ 201	£ 991
06/09/02	32	46	£ 1,920	£ 2,300	£ 182	£ 853
07/09/02	20	13	£ 1,200	£ 650	£ 156	£ 520
Totals			**£ 16,620**	**£ 15,350**	**£ 1,445**	**£ 6,001**

£ 50.00 Cost per night of standard room
£ 60.00 Cost per night of luxury room

Figure 12.15 Part of Report 1 for Grand Hotel

The line graph in Report 3 should have four lines, one each for luxury rooms, standard rooms, bar takings and restaurant.

Outcomes matching guide

Outcome 1: *Design a spreadsheet to meet a given specification*	
Practical activities The candidate will be able to	
1 Create a data capture form to facilitate data input	Section 2 Tasks 2.1 to 2.10 Section 8 Task 8.5

2 Identify data in a spreadsheet specification
    • data to be input
    • data generated while processing
    • output data required
	Section 2 Information: Input, processing and output

3 Plan a spreadsheet structure to include • data labels, column and row titles	Section 2 Task 2.1 Section 8 Task 8.1
• hidden and/or protected cells	Section 2 Task 2.10 Section 3 Task 3.10
• cell naming, absolute and relative cell references	Section 4 Tasks 4.5 to 4.10
• header/footer information	Section 3 Task 3.13
4 Use suitable formats for data • alignment: left, centre, right	Section 2 Task 2.5 Section 8 Task 8.2
• text enhancements	Section 2 Task 2.3
• cell attributes: size, borders, background	Section 2 Tasks 2.2, 2.8, 2.9
• numbers: general, fixed, percentage, currency, date/time	Section 2 Task 2.4
5 Perform calculations using formulas • maximum	Section 4 Task 4.1
• minimum	Section 4 Task 4.1
• count	Section 4 Task 4.2
• round	Section 4 Task 4.2
• date	Section 4 Task 4.2
6 Create and use simple IF statements	Section 4 Tasks 4.11, 4.14
7 Calculate the result of a simple IF statement	Section 4 Information: IF functions and relational operators
8 Define the printout required for a given application • page size and orientation	Section 7 Task 7.3
• margins, multi-page or fit-to-page	Section 7 Tasks 7.2, 7.3
• headers and footers	Section 3 Task 3.13
9 Create test data to validate the spreadsheet with associated results of independent calculations • representative, marginal, rogue and extreme values	Section 4 Information: Choosing data for testing formulas Section 8 Task 8.4

Underpinning knowledge	
1 Describe the need for accuracy in design, data input and clear output	Section 4 Information: Using formulas and functions
2 Distinguish between input data, output data and data processing, in spreadsheets	Section 2 Information: Input, processing and output
3 Identify the kinds of data that should be protected and/or hidden in a spreadsheet	Section 2 Information: Protecting spreadsheets and unlocking cells Section 3 Task 3.10
4 Describe how the design of the spreadsheet and the accuracy of data input impact on the output data	Section 2 Information: Input, processing and output Section 4 Information: Using formulas and functions

Outcome 2: Create and test a simple spreadsheet	
Practical activities The candidate will be able to	
1 Create a spreadsheet according to a given design • enter titles and headings	Section 2 Task 2.1
• enter formulas, functions and constant data	Section 1 Task 1.2 Section 4 Tasks 4.1, 4.2
• format columns, rows and cells appropriately	Section 2 Tasks 2.2 to 2.9
2 Improve and adjust design to facilitate data entry and output	Section 8 Information and Task 8.6
3 Insert, delete, clear: cells, rows and columns	Section 3 Tasks 3.6, 3.7
4 Move and copy cell data, formulas and formats	Section 3 Tasks 3.2 to 3.5
5 Use search and replace to edit data/formulas	Section 3 Task 3.9
6 Use split/freeze window to retain column and row heading visibility	Section 3 Tasks 3.11, 3.12
7 Test a spreadsheet • input test data and compare results with expected outcomes • rectify errors in design or in design implementation	Section 4 Tasks 4.13, 4.15
8 Set a spreadsheet to show formulas	Section 4 Task 4.3
9 Hide and/or protect cells	Section 2 Task 2.10 Section 3 Task 3.10
Underpinning knowledge	
1 Identify the advantages of using freeze panes, screen borders and windows	Section 3 Tasks 3.11, 3.12
2 Describe commonly used cell formats and relate them to typical numeric data used	Section 2 Information: Number formats
3 Define the relational operators equal to (=), greater than (>), less than (<)	Section 4 Information: Relational operators

Outcome 3: Link, import and extract data

Practical activities
The candidate will be able to

1	Copy values and formulas from one spreadsheet into another	Section 6 Tasks 6.5, 6.6, 6.10
2	Create cell references that link spreadsheets	Section 6 Tasks 6.7, 6.11
3	Create new spreadsheets from sections of existing spreadsheets	Section 6 Tasks 6.5 to 6.11 Information: Importing and extracting data
4	Save edited spreadsheets	Section 1 Task 1.5 Section 6 Information: Importing and extracting data

Outcome 4: Produce graphs and charts

Practical activities
The candidate will be able to

1	Select and use chart type to suit data • pie – single data series 100% • bar – grouped/discrete data – especially comparing size • column – grouped/discrete data – especially showing time variation • line – continuous data, trends at equal intervals • XY & scatter – dependent and independent values, unequal intervals	Section 5 Information: Choosing the right chart, Tasks 5.1, 5.3, 5.10 to 5.14
2	Format chart information to suit data • titles and axes labels • axes scales and limits • gridlines and gridline density • legends and data labels	Section 5 Tasks 5.1, 5.7, 5.8
3	Format chart aesthetically by changing • background • line, area and text attributes • chart size relative to spreadsheet • colours to suit monochrome/colour output	Section 5 Tasks 5.4, 5.8

Underpinning knowledge

1	Identify reasons why different types of chart are suited to different types of data	Section 5 Information: Choosing the right chart

Outcome 5: Export and print spreadsheets

Practical activities
The candidate will be able to

1	Print out spreadsheets • monochrome/colour printing facilities	Section 7 Task 7.7
	• selected areas or whole sheet	Section 7 Task 7.6
	• as single charts	Section 5 Tasks 5.2, 5.5
	• using borders	Section 2 Task 2.8
	• with/without headers and footers	Section 3 Task 3.13
	• fit to one page	Section 7 Task 7.3

• with/without repeated table headings	Section 3 Task 3.14
• including/excluding graphics	Section 5 Task 5.5 Section 7 Task 7.5
• values/formulas	Section 4 Task 4.3
2 Export data or graphic to another spreadsheet file	Section 6 Tasks 6.10 to 6.13
Underpinning knowledge	
1 Identify the differences between copying data values, linking data values and pasting data objects	Section 6 Information: Copying, copying values only and linking Tasks 6.10 to 6.13

Quick reference guide

This includes some keyboard shortcuts (hotkeys).

Any drop down menu can be displayed by holding down the Alt key as you press the key for the letter that is underlined in the menu name. For example, Alt + f displays the File menu. Each command in the menu has an underlined letter. Type the letter to carry out the command.

A right mouse click on a cell, selection or object will produce a pop-up menu of available commands.

Managing folders, files, workbooks and worksheets

Create a new folder
Starting from the Excel Save dialogue box – click the Create New Folder button and name the folder.
Starting from a folder on the Windows desktop – File menu, New then Folder. Name the folder.

Create a new workbook file
Click the New toolbar button. Or File menu, New, then click OK in the dialogue box. Or hotkey Ctrl + n.

Open a workbook file
Click the Open toolbar button. Or File menu, Open. Or hotkey Ctrl + o. Then navigate to the file in the Open dialogue box, select the file and click Open.

Save a workbook file
Click the Save toolbar button. Or File menu, Save. Or hotkey Ctrl + s.

Save a second copy of a workbook with another name or in another place
File menu, Save As. Choose the folder, name the file, click Save.

Switch between open workbooks
Click on the workbook's button on the taskbar at the bottom of the screen.
Or Window menu and select the name of the workbook.
Or hotkey Ctrl + Tab until you reach the workbook you want.

Switch between worksheets in a workbook
Click on the worksheet tab near the bottom of the window.
Or hotkeys Ctrl + Page Up and Ctrl + Page Down.

Move a worksheet
Drag the worksheet tab to its new position in the same or another workbook.
Or right click the worksheet tab, select Move or Copy and choose the new position.

Copy a worksheet
Hold down the Ctrl key as you drag the worksheet tab to its new position.
Or right click the worksheet tab, select Move or Copy, tick the Create a Copy box and choose the new position. Click OK.

Close a workbook
Click the X close button in the top right of the workbook window. (This is the lower X if there are two. The upper X is the button to close Excel.)
Or File menu, Close. Or hotkey Ctrl + w.

Enter, edit, delete, insert, search, undo

Enter cell contents
Select the cell with the mouse or cursor (arrow) keys. Key in the data. Press Enter to complete entry and move down.
Or press Tab to complete entry and move right.
Or press Shift + Enter to complete entry and move up.
Or click the green tick in the formula bar to complete entry and stay in the same cell.
To cancel an entry before completion, press Esc or click the red cross in the formula bar.

Edit cell contents	To replace an existing entry, select the cell and key in the new entry. To alter the existing entry, double click in the cell to place a cursor and edit in the cell. Or click into the formula bar and edit the active cell there. Or use the F2 function key to place a cursor and edit the active cell as before.
Delete cell contents	Edit menu, Clear, then choose Contents to clear contents but leave formatting, or choose All to clear both contents and formatting. The Delete key clears the content but not the formatting and completes the action. The Backspace delete key clears the content but leaves the cursor in the cell instead of completing the action. When editing cell contents, Backspace deletes to the left and Delete deletes to the right.
Insert a row or column	Insert menu, Rows or Columns. Or use a keyboard shortcut Ctrl + Shift + + (plus key) and choose to insert a row or a column. If a whole row or column is selected then the insertion will happen at once. If several rows or columns are selected then that number of rows or columns will be inserted.
Delete a row or column	Edit menu, Delete. Choose to delete a whole row or column or to shift cells up or left. If you select a whole row or column before using Edit, Delete then the whole row or column will be deleted.
Search for text in a cell	Edit menu, Find. Or hotkey Ctrl + f. Key in text, set options and click Find Next.
Replace text in a cell	Edit menu, Replace. Or hotkey Ctrl + h. Key in text to find and replace, set options and click Find Next, then Replace.
Undo actions	Click the Undo toolbar button to undo the last action. The arrow by the button gives a list of actions so that you can undo several at once. Or Edit button, Undo … The most recent action will be shown. Or hotkey Ctrl + z.

Formulas, functions and testing

Basic arithmetic operations	Start formula with =. Use the operators + (add) − (subtract) * (multiply) / (divide).
Mixed operations	Brackets first, then multiply and divide, then add and subtract.
SUM()	Adds the contents of cells and ranges in its brackets. Key in the formula or click the Autosum toolbar button or hotkey Alt + =.
AVERAGE()	Finds the average (mean) of cells and ranges in its brackets.
MAX()	Finds the largest value in the cells and ranges in its brackets.
MIN()	Finds the smallest value in the cells and ranges in its brackets.
TODAY()	Returns the current date.
ROUND()	Needs two numbers in its brackets: the number to be rounded and the number of decimal places to keep.
COUNT()	Finds how many of the cells in the brackets contain numbers.
IF()	Has three entries (arguments) in its brackets. A condition that may be true or false, the action to take if true, the action to take if false.
Relative and absolute references	When formulas are copied, relative references change to suit their new position, absolute references do not change. Absolute references are shown by dollar signs, e.g. $A$4.

Named cells and ranges	To name a selected cell or range, click the Insert menu, select Name, then select Define. Key in the name. OK.
	Named cells in formulas are unchanged when copied, like absolute references.
Choosing test data	Use representative data, extreme data and rogue data. Also use marginal values to test formulas containing IF functions.

Formats

Number formats	Currency and percent can be set using toolbar buttons or just by keying in a number as currency or percent. Number of decimal places can be increased or decreased using toolbar buttons. To set other number formats, Format menu, Cells, Number tab.
Date formats	Date formats are set automatically if you key in a date. To set Date formats, Format menu, Cells, Number tab. Date formats can be used for medium and long dates. Short dates have the month first. Use the Custom format dd/mm/yy to put the day first.
Font, size and enhancements	Use the toolbar lists and buttons for font, size, bold, italic or underline.
	Or click the Format menu, Cells then click the Font tab and select the options from the dialogue box.
	Or use keyboard shortcuts: Ctrl + b for bold, Ctrl + i for italic, Ctrl + u for underline.
	Ctrl + 1 (number one, not letter L) shows the Format cells dialogue box.
Borders	Select cells and use the toolbar button and drop down list for common border patterns.
	Or click the Format menu, Cells then click the Border tab for more options.
Background fills and patterns	Select cells and use the toolbar button and drop down list for coloured fills.
	Or click the Format menu, Cells then click the Patterns tab for more options.
Locking and protection	Click the Format menu, Cells then click the Protection tab and unlock selected cells. Then click the Tools menu, Protection to protect the sheet. A password is optional.

Moving, copying and linking cell contents, values, formulas and formats

Cut command	Toolbar Cut button or Edit menu, Cut or keyboard shortcut Ctrl + x.
Copy command	Toolbar Copy button or Edit menu, Copy or keyboard shortcut Ctrl + c.
Paste command	Toolbar Paste button or Edit menu, Paste or keyboard shortcut Ctrl + v.
Move cell contents	Select cells, cut, move to new position, paste.
	Or point to cell border, hold down the left mouse button and drag to new position.
Copy cell contents	Select cells, copy, move to new position, paste.
	Or point to cell border, hold down the left mouse button and hold down Ctrl key as you drag to new position
Copy values only	Select cells, copy, move to new position. Edit menu, Paste. Special – values.

Copy formats only	Select cells, copy, move to new position. Edit menu, Paste. Special – formats.
Link cells	Select cells, copy, move to new position. Edit menu, Paste. Special – Paste Link.

Printing and screen display

Print a worksheet	Preview first. Click the Print Preview toolbar button. Or File menu, Print Preview. Click the Print button in the Preview window. To print without previewing, use the toolbar Print button or the hotkey Ctrl + p.
Print a selected area	As a one-off, File menu, Print, choose the Selection option, click OK. For long-term use, File menu, Print Area then Set Print Area. Print as usual.
Show gridlines, row numbers and column letters for printing	File menu, Page Setup, Sheet tab, click Gridlines and Row and Column headings.
Repeat selected cells on each page	File menu, Page Setup, Sheet tab, choose rows or columns to repeat.
Show/Hide formulas	Tools menu, Options, View tab. Click in Formulas box. Or Ctrl + ' (backwards quote).
Show/hide objects	Tools menu, Options, View tab. Objects row, choose show all or hide all.
Page orientation	File menu, Page Setup, Page tab, Portrait or Landscape.
Fit on one page	File menu, Page Setup, Page tab, Fit to 1 page wide by 1 page tall.
Add headers and footers	View menu, Headers and Footers. Or File menu, Page Setup, Header/Footer tab.
Split window	Select position to split. Window menu, Split.
Freeze panes	Select position to freeze. Window menu, Freeze panes.
Arrange windows (for 2 or more workbooks)	Window menu, Arrange. Choose horizontal or vertical.

Charts

Create a chart	Select the data. Click the Chart Wizard toolbar button. Or Insert menu, Chart.
Move and resize a chart on a worksheet	Point to outer area and drag to move. Use resize handles to make larger or smaller.
Format a chart	Double click on area required. Or right click and select Format… Select required options from dialogue box.
Print a chart	To print chart alone, select chart before printing. Deselect chart to print whole sheet.